Real World
Colouring Book
For Advanced Users & Adults

50 Images

**Created From Real Life Photos
For You To Colour As You Please.**

ISBN 978-0-359-97227-2
90000
9 780359 972272

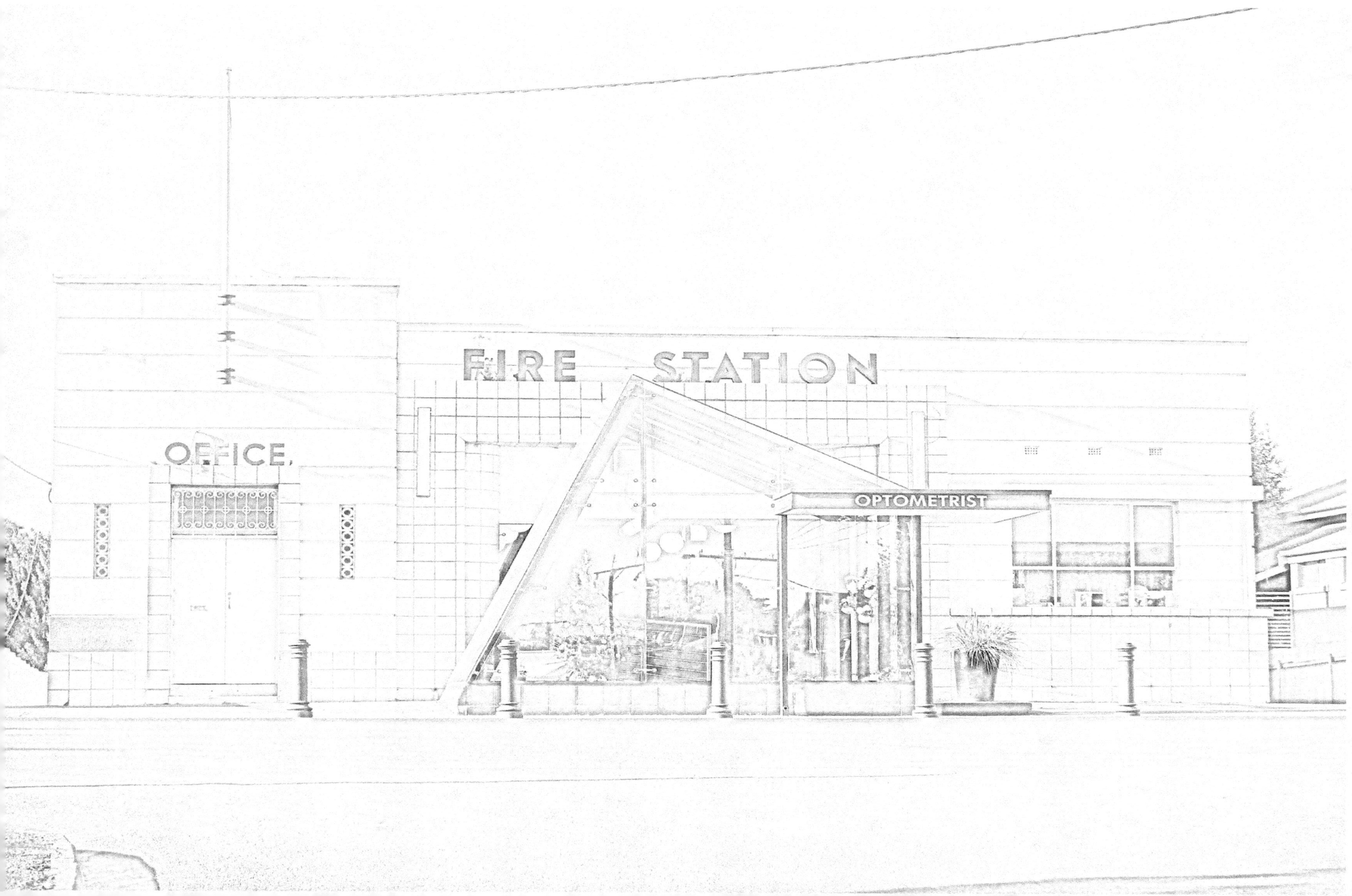

FIRE STATION
OFFICE
OPTOMETRIST

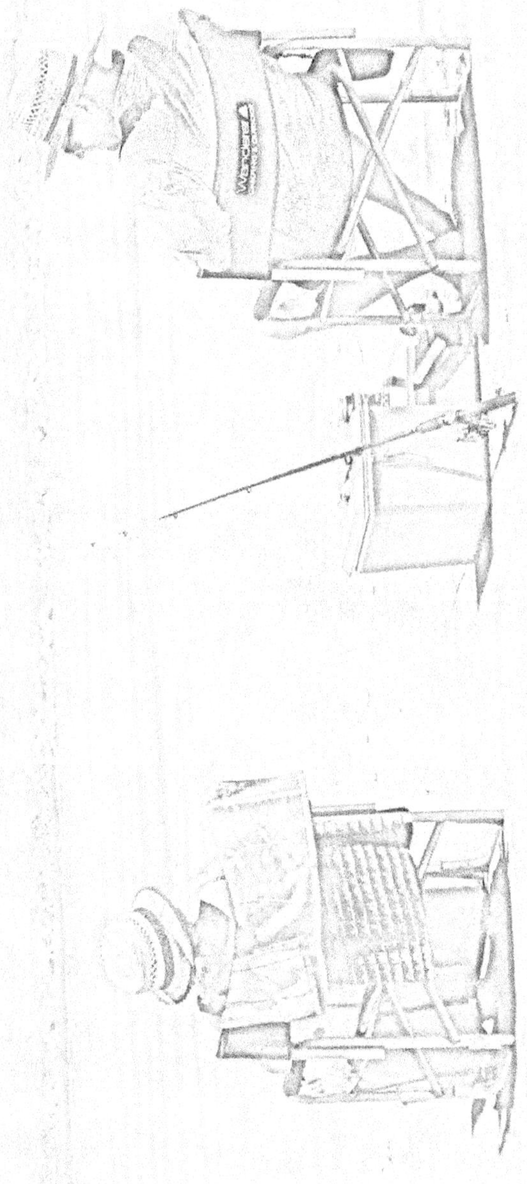

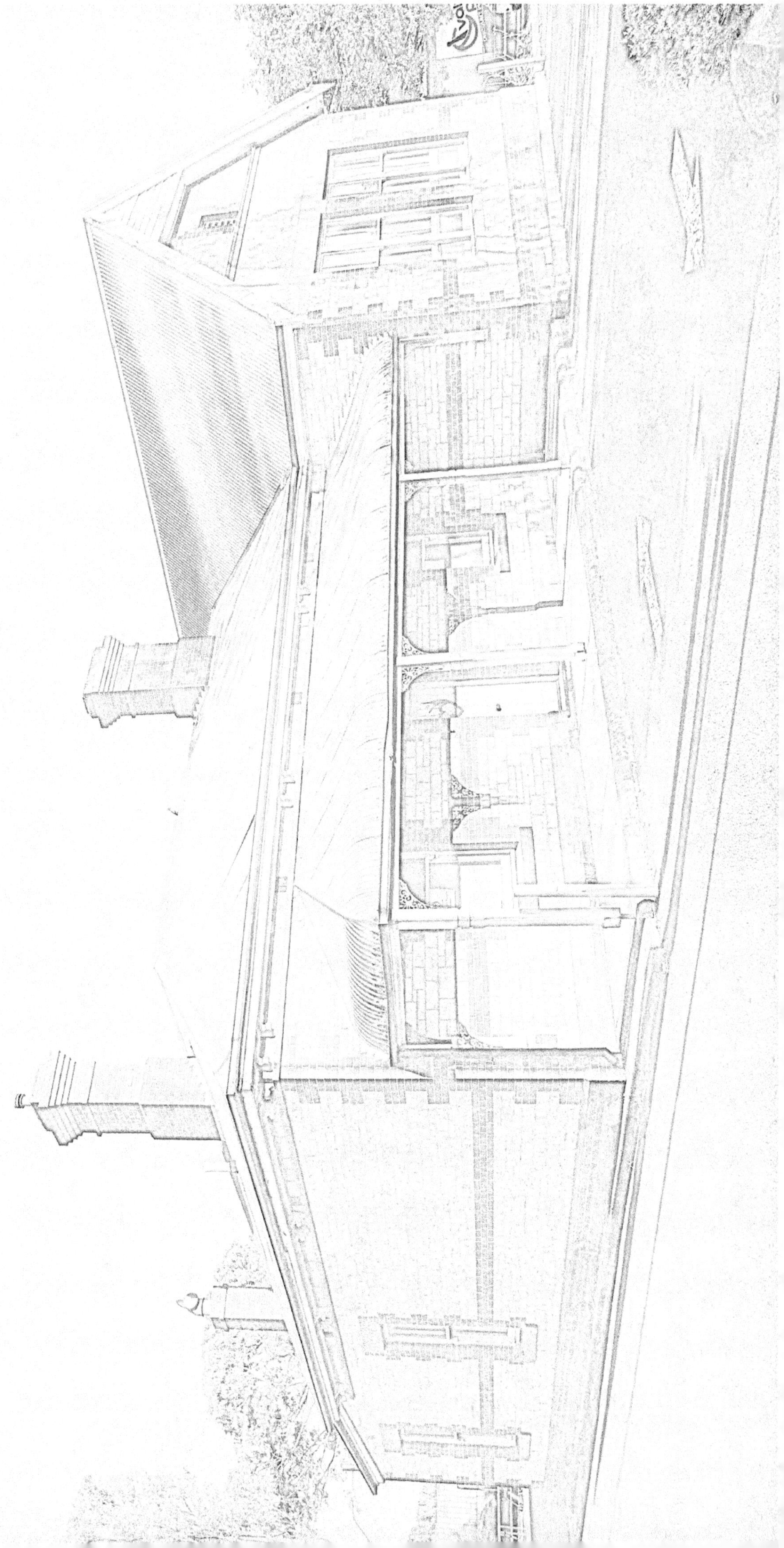

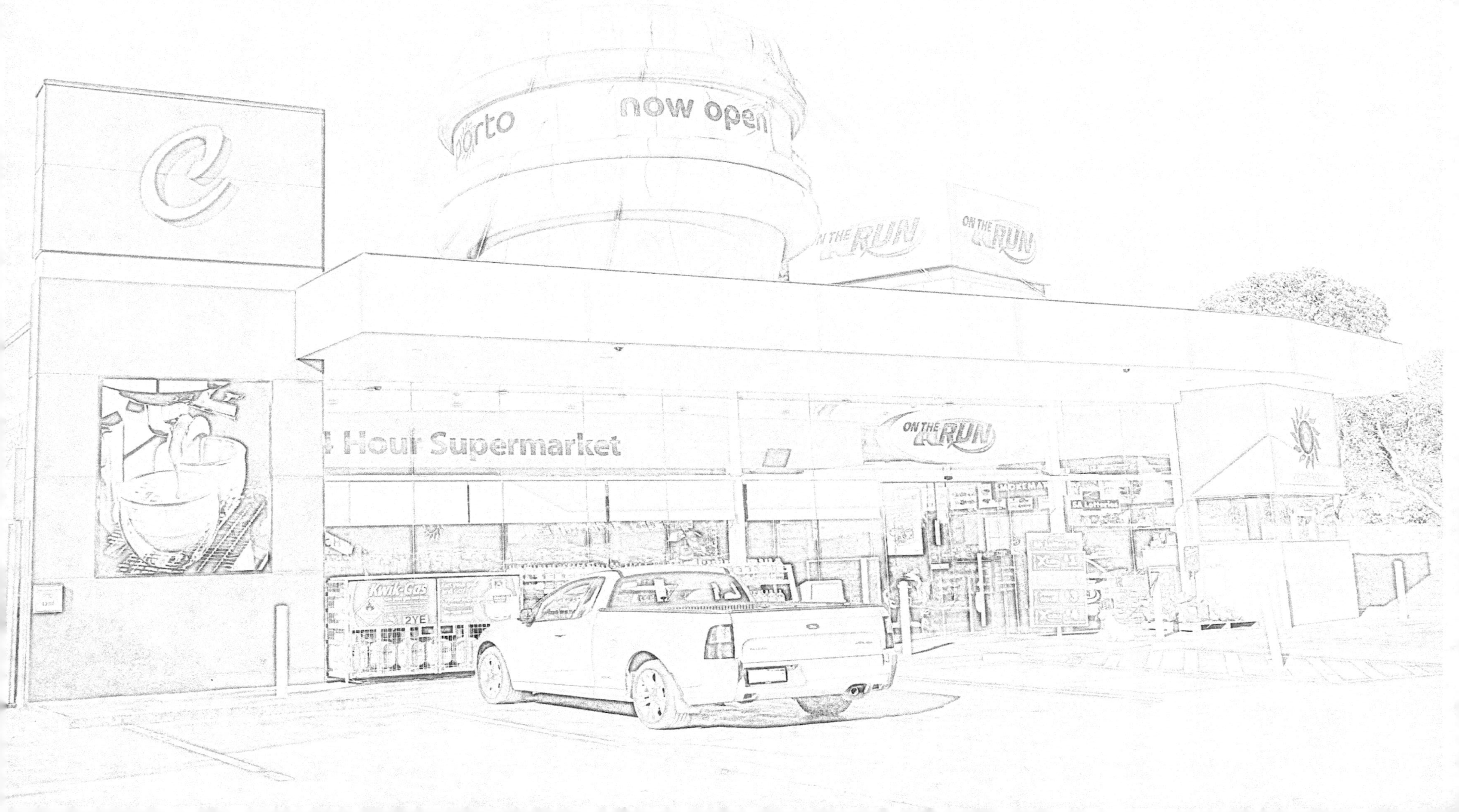

now open
ON THE RUN
ON THE RUN
Hour Supermarket
ON THE RUN
SMOKEMA
Kwik-Gas
2YE

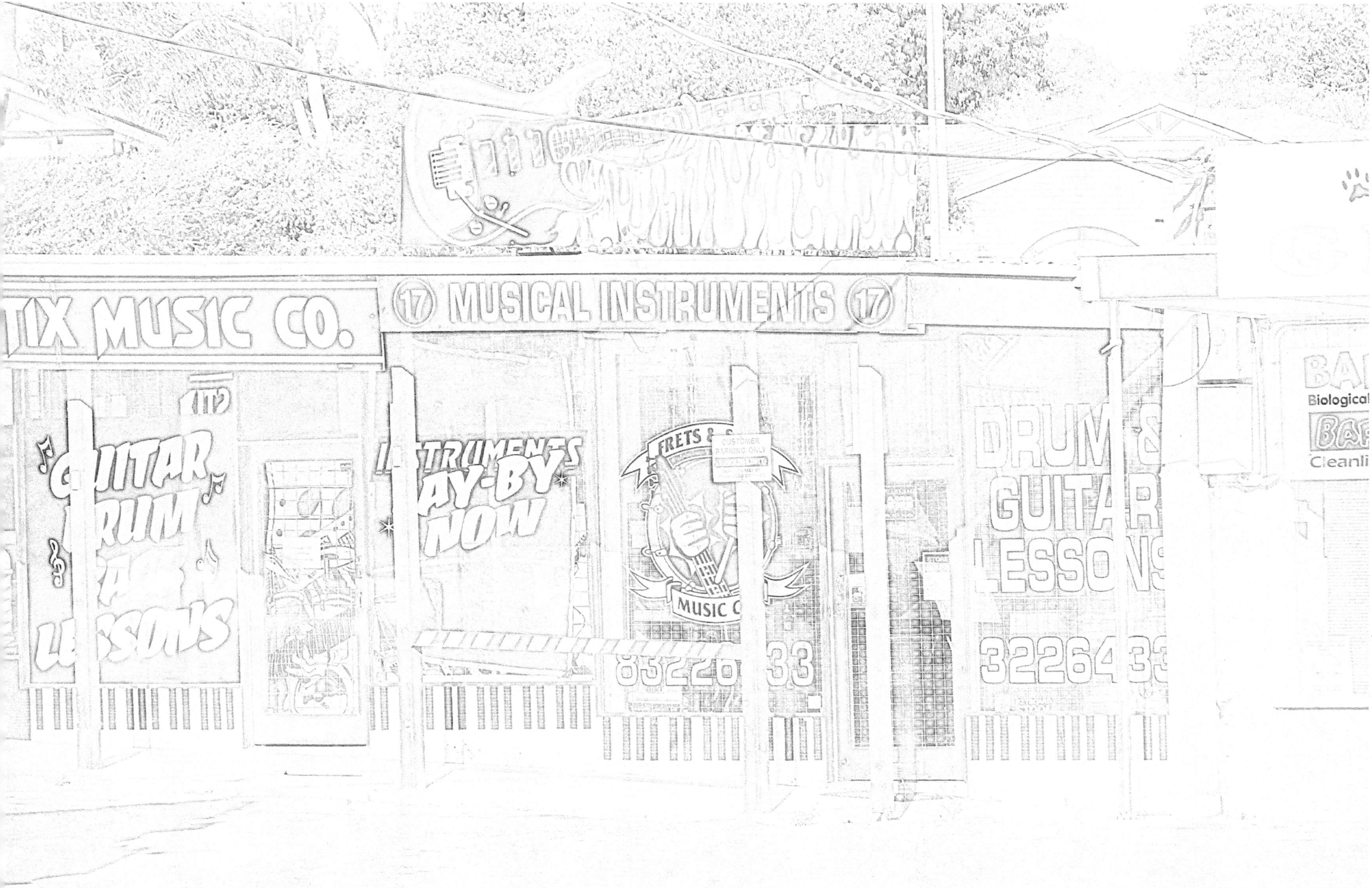

TIX MUSIC CO.
17 MUSICAL INSTRUMENTS 17
LESSONS
NOW
CUSTOMER PARKING ONLY
MUSIC C
DRUM &
GUITAR
LESSONS
Biological
Cleanli

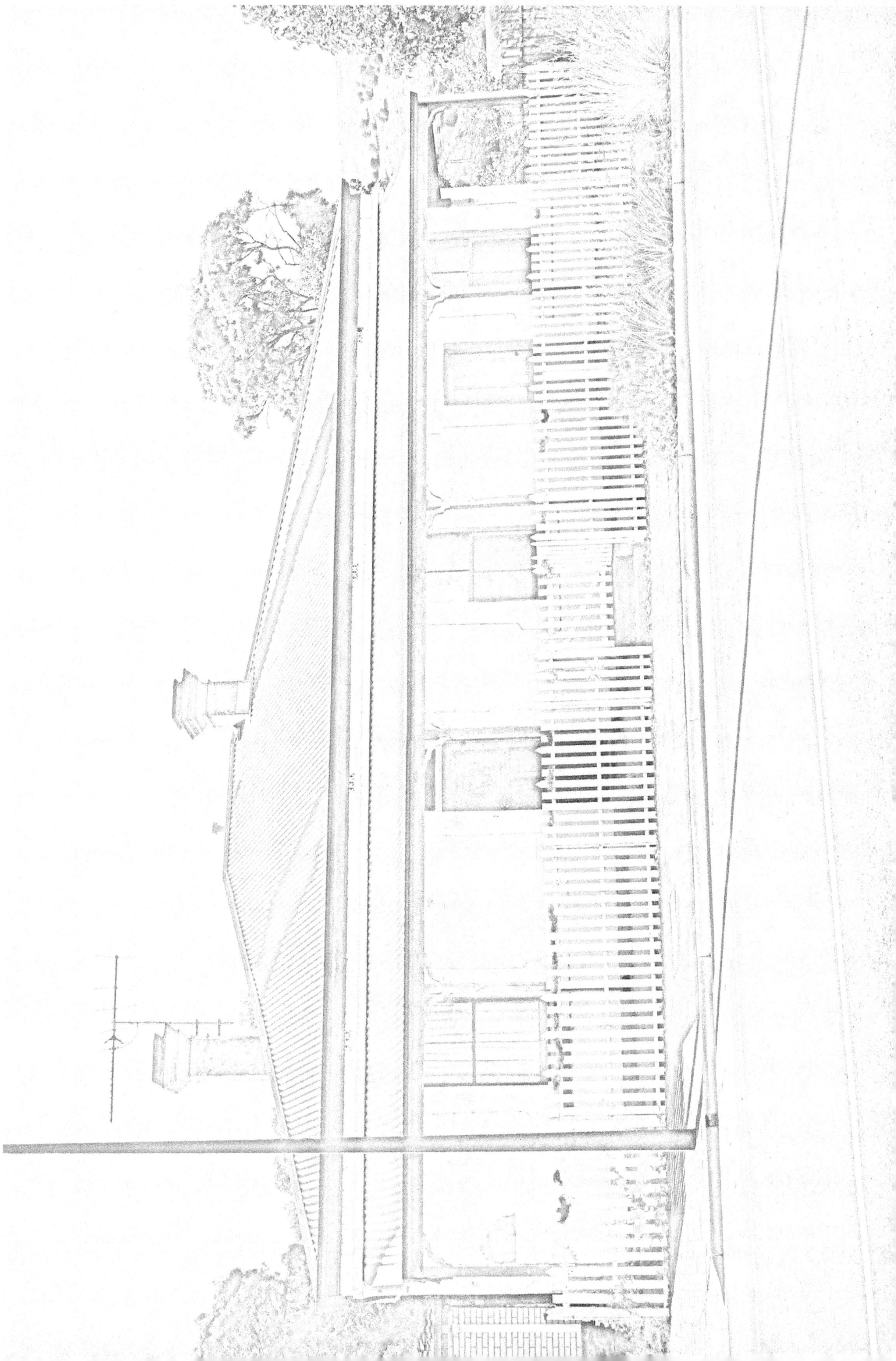

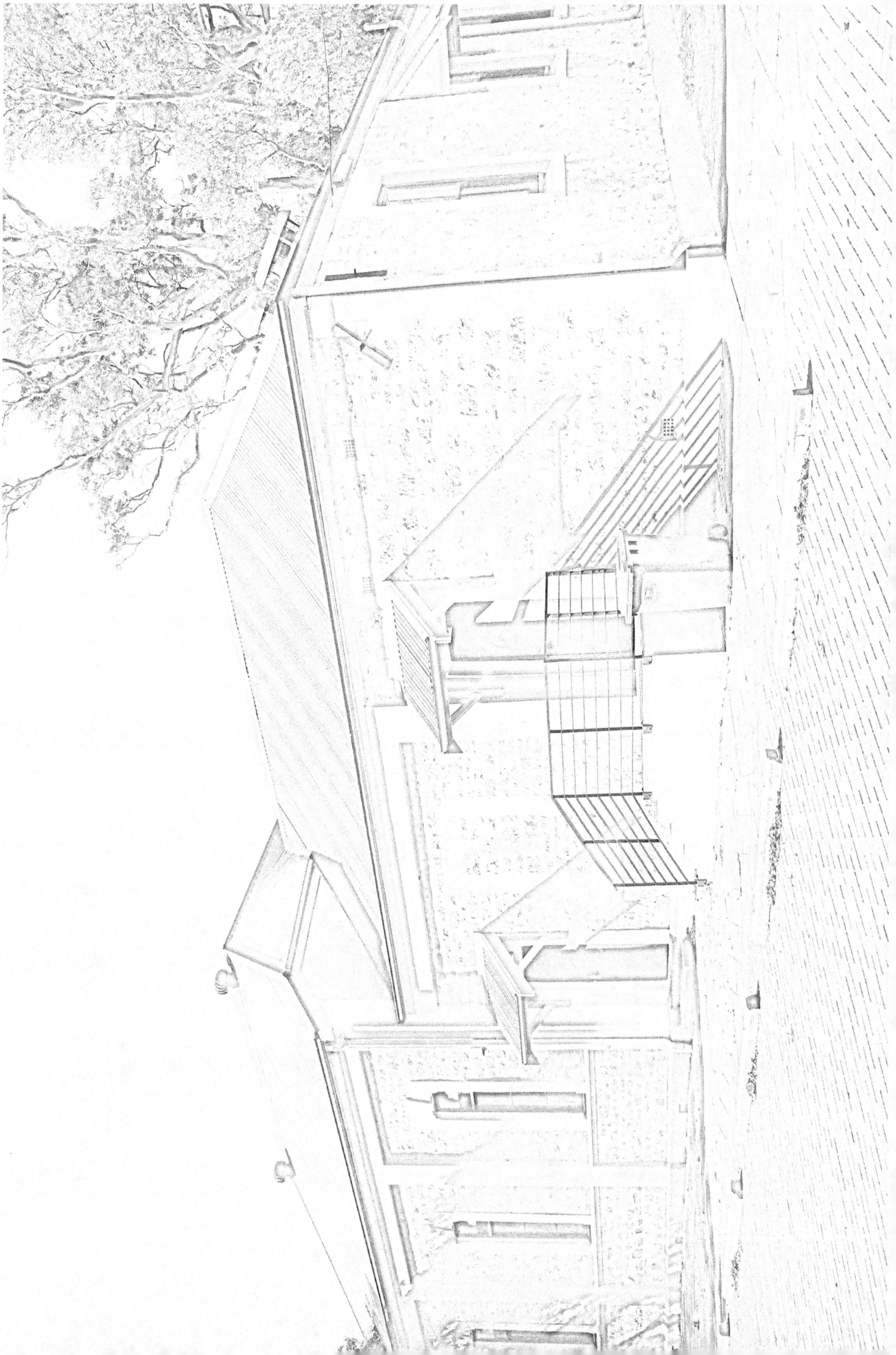

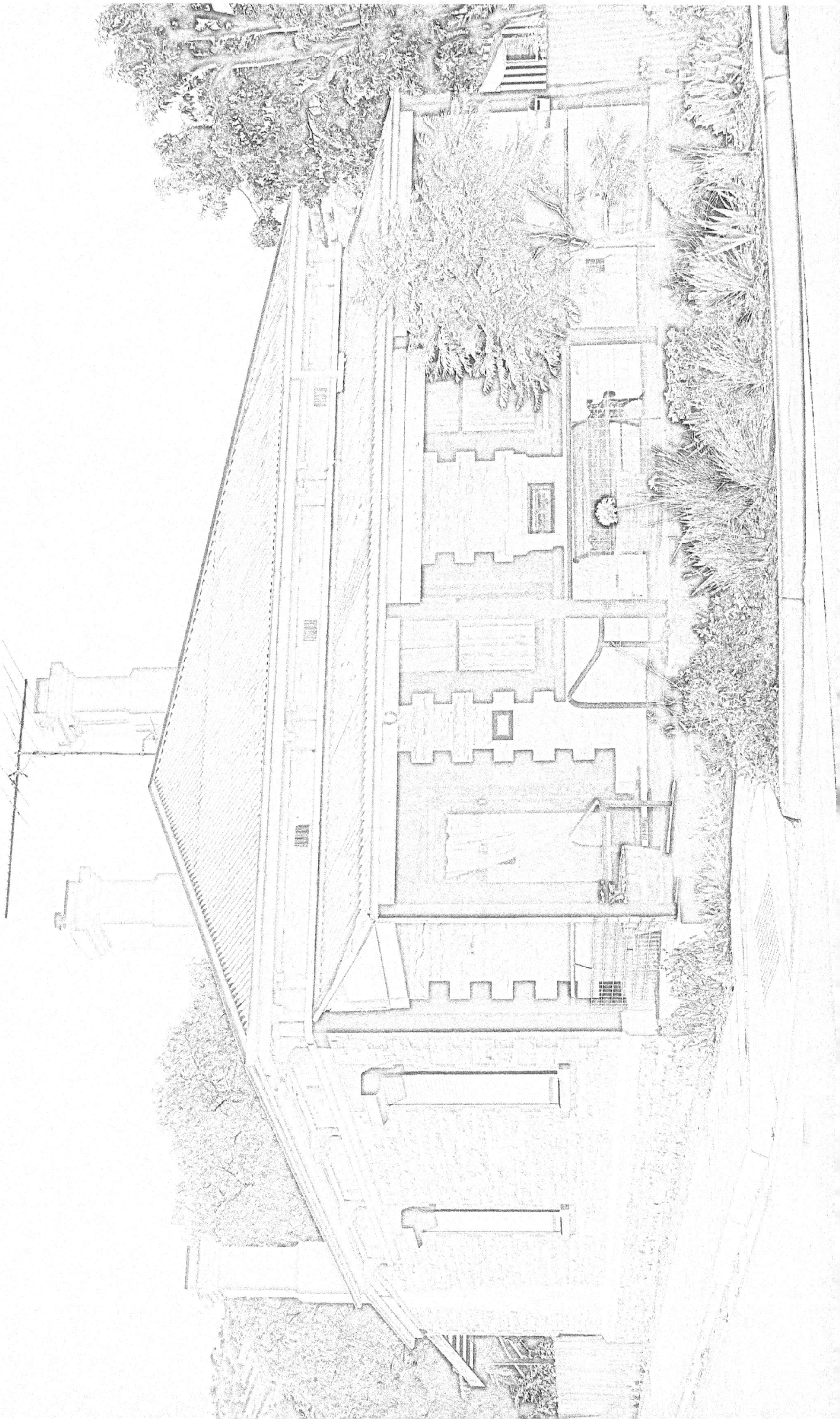

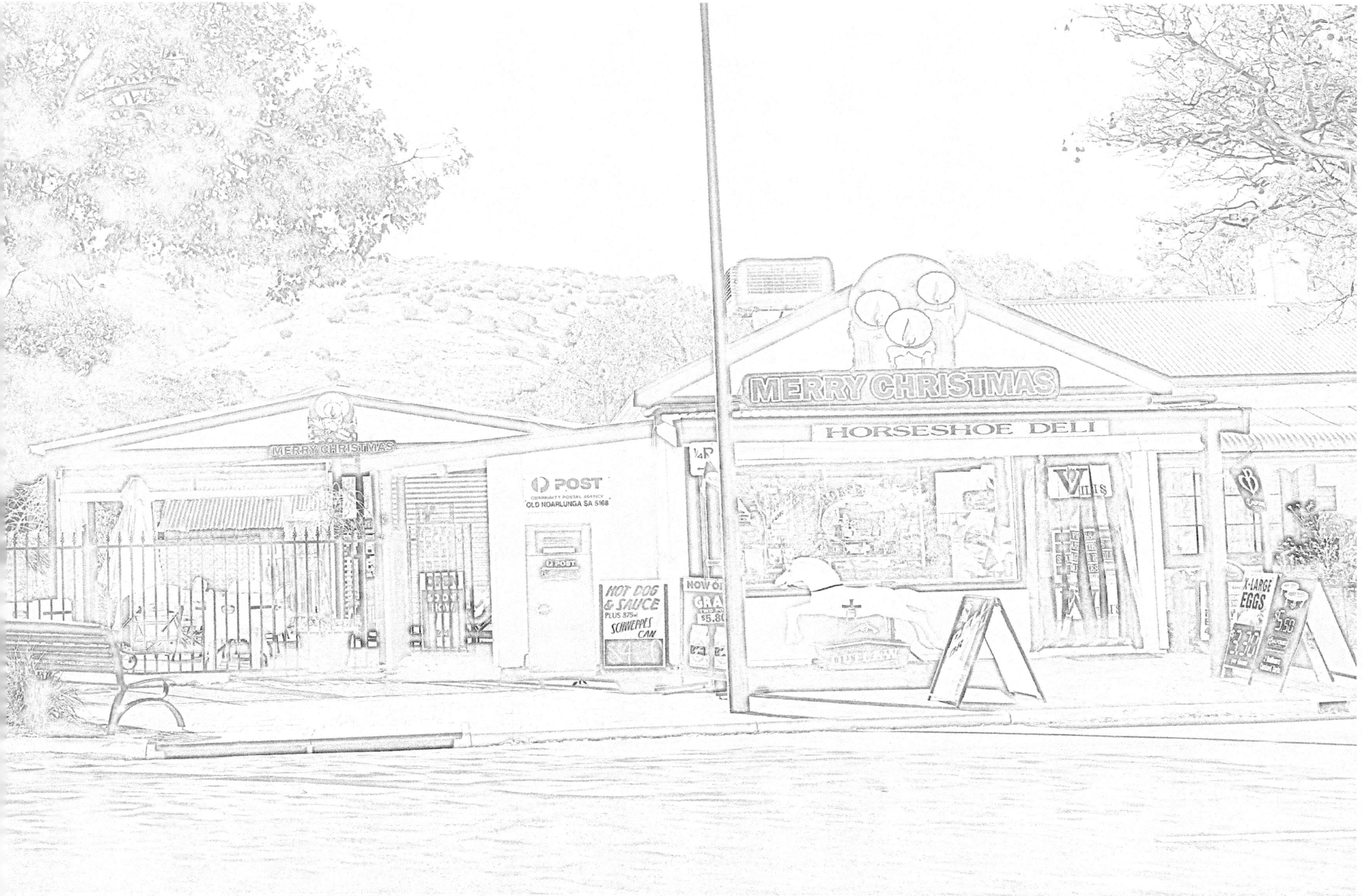
MERRY CHRISTMAS
HORSESHOE DELI
MERRY CHRISTMAS
POST
COMMUNITY POSTAL AGENCY
OLD NOARLUNGA SA 5168
POST
HOT DOG & SAUCE
PLUS 375ml
SCHWEPPES CAN
X-LARGE EGGS

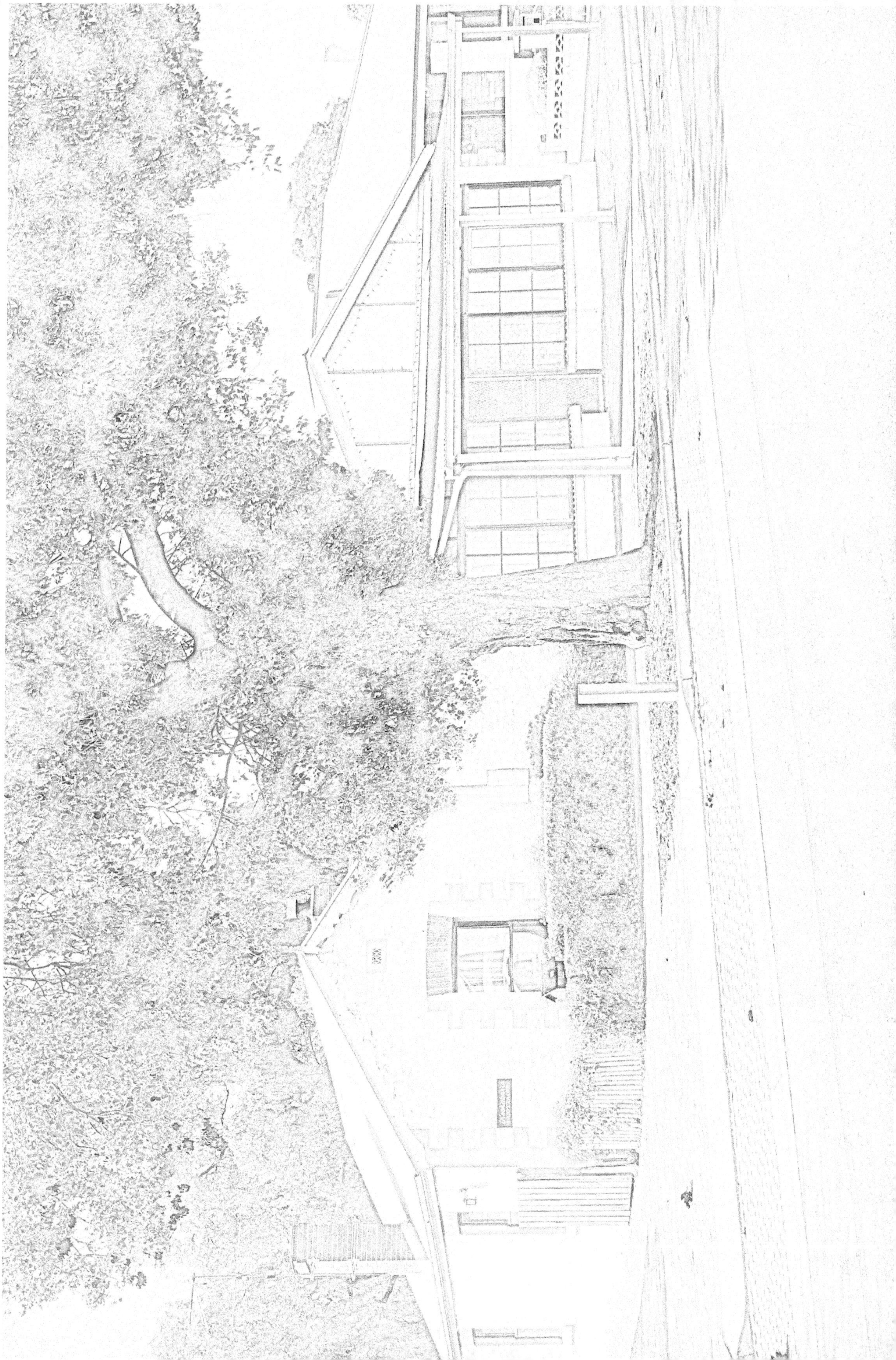

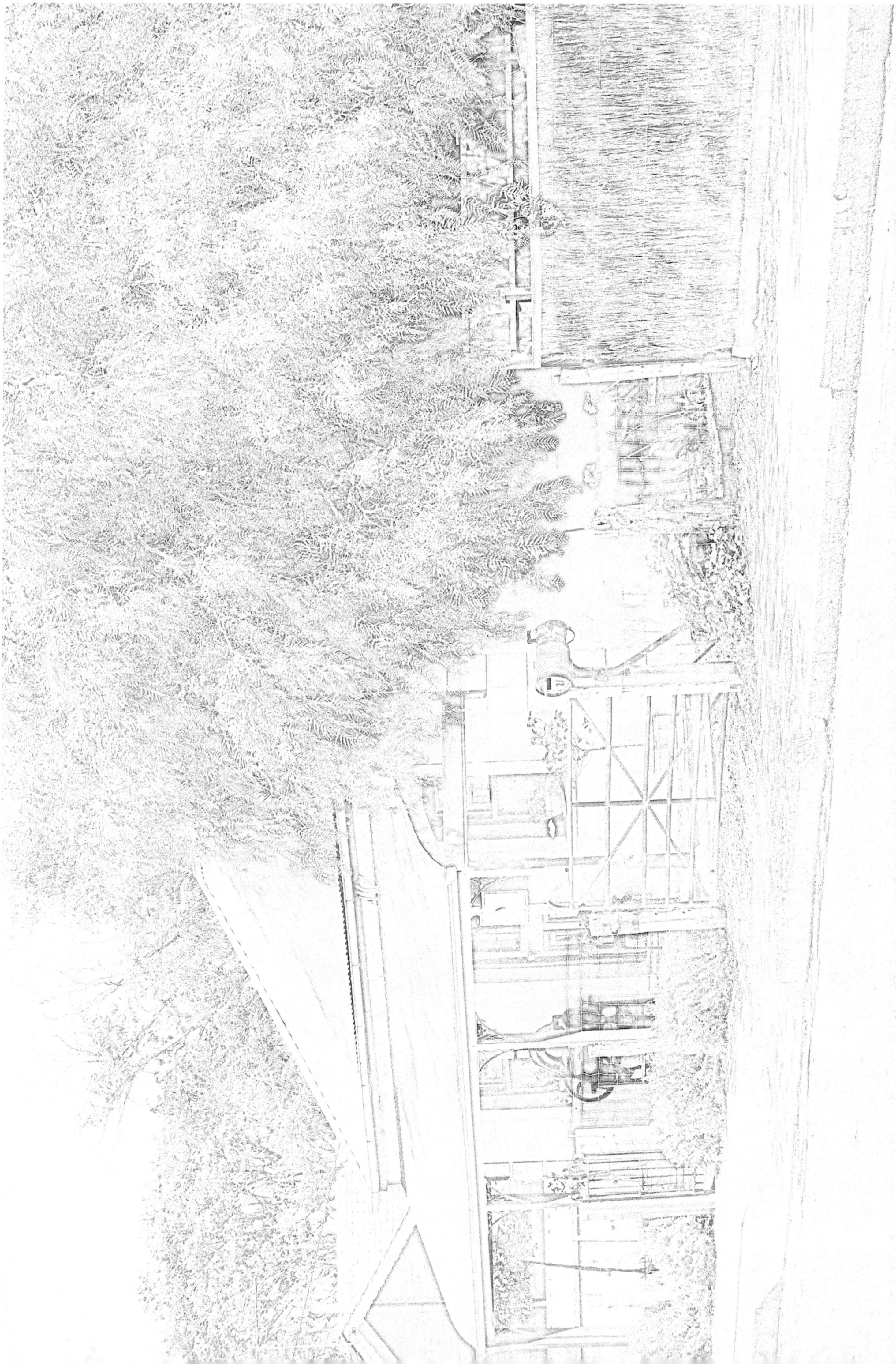

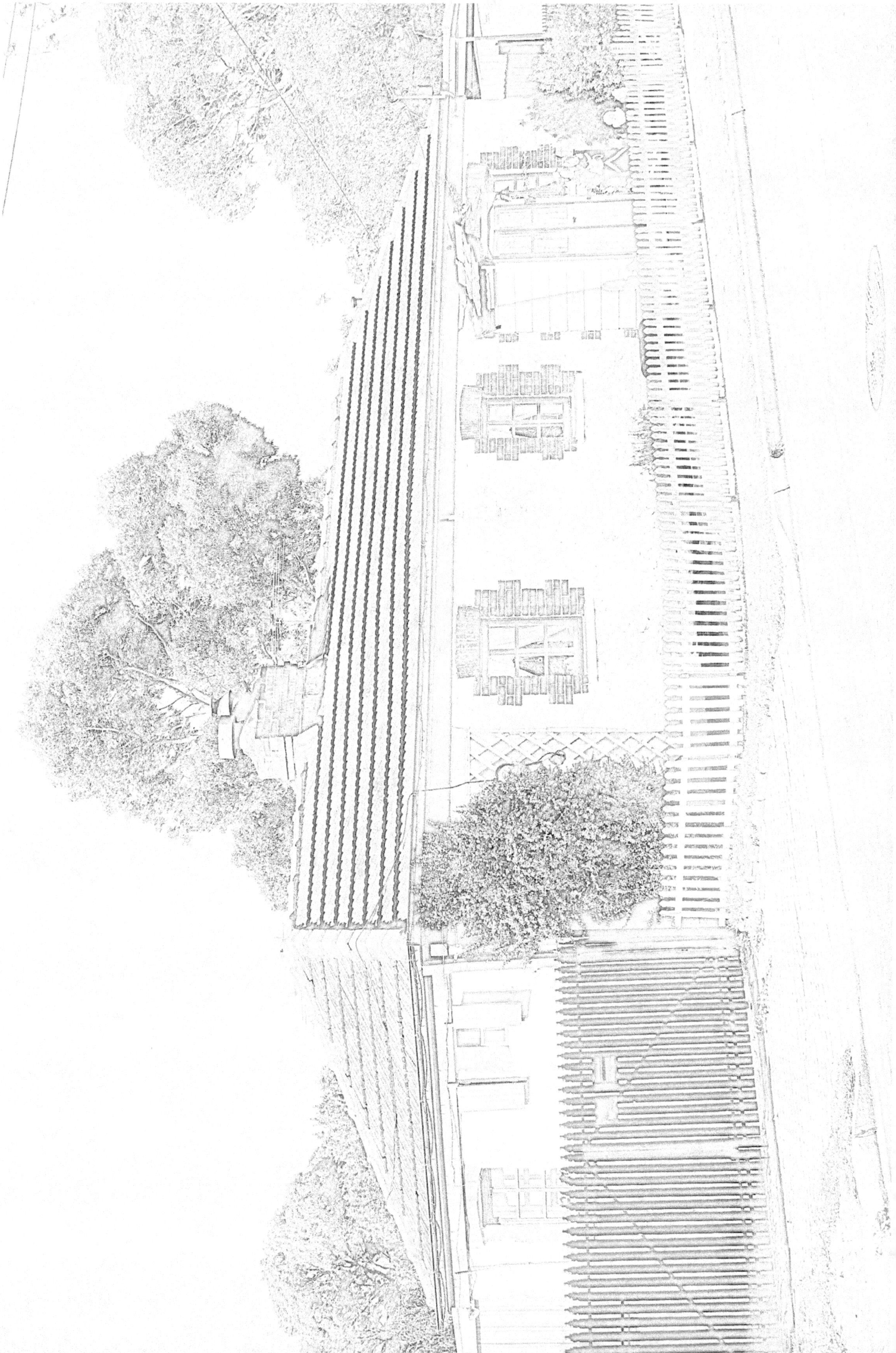

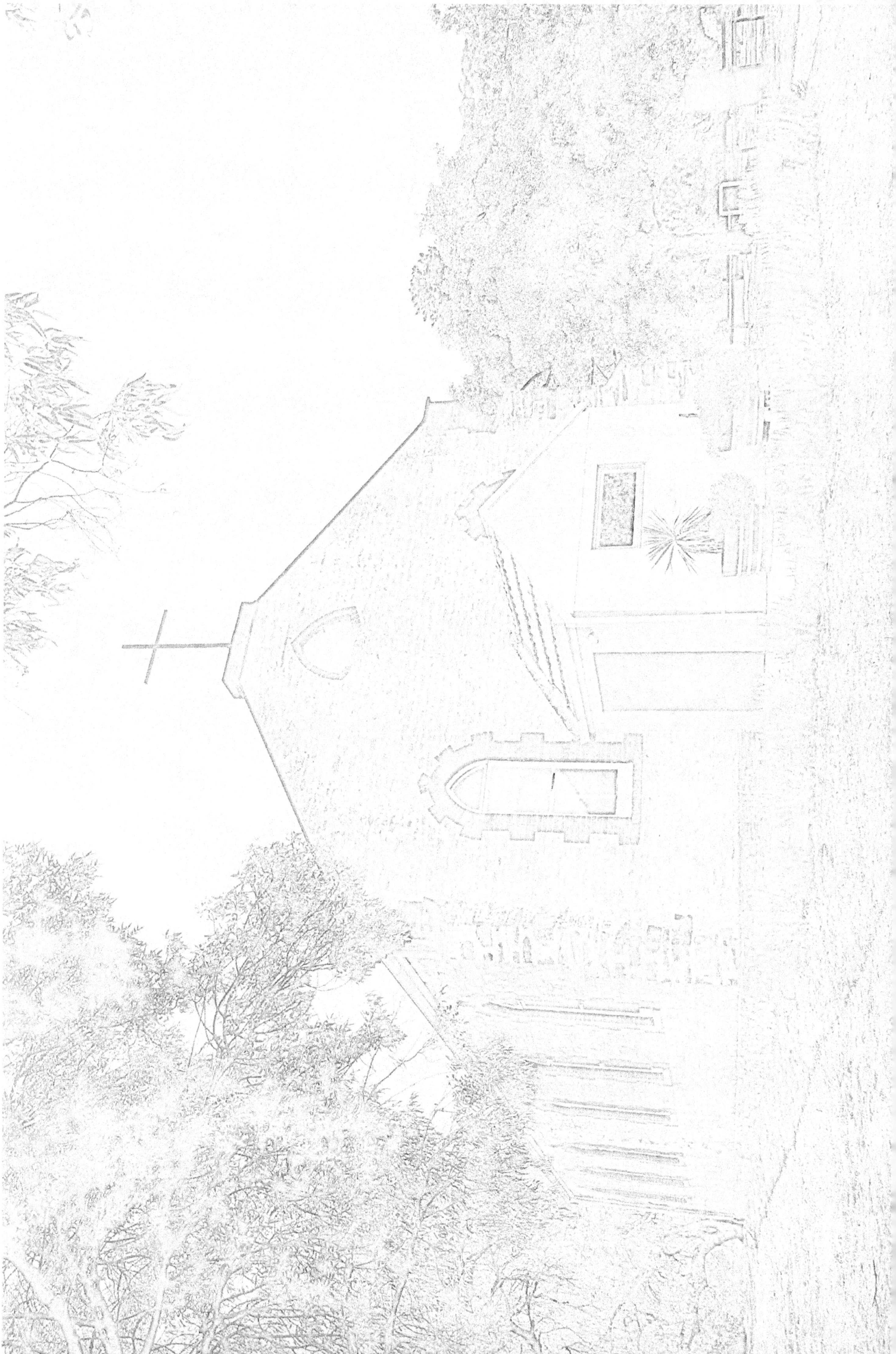

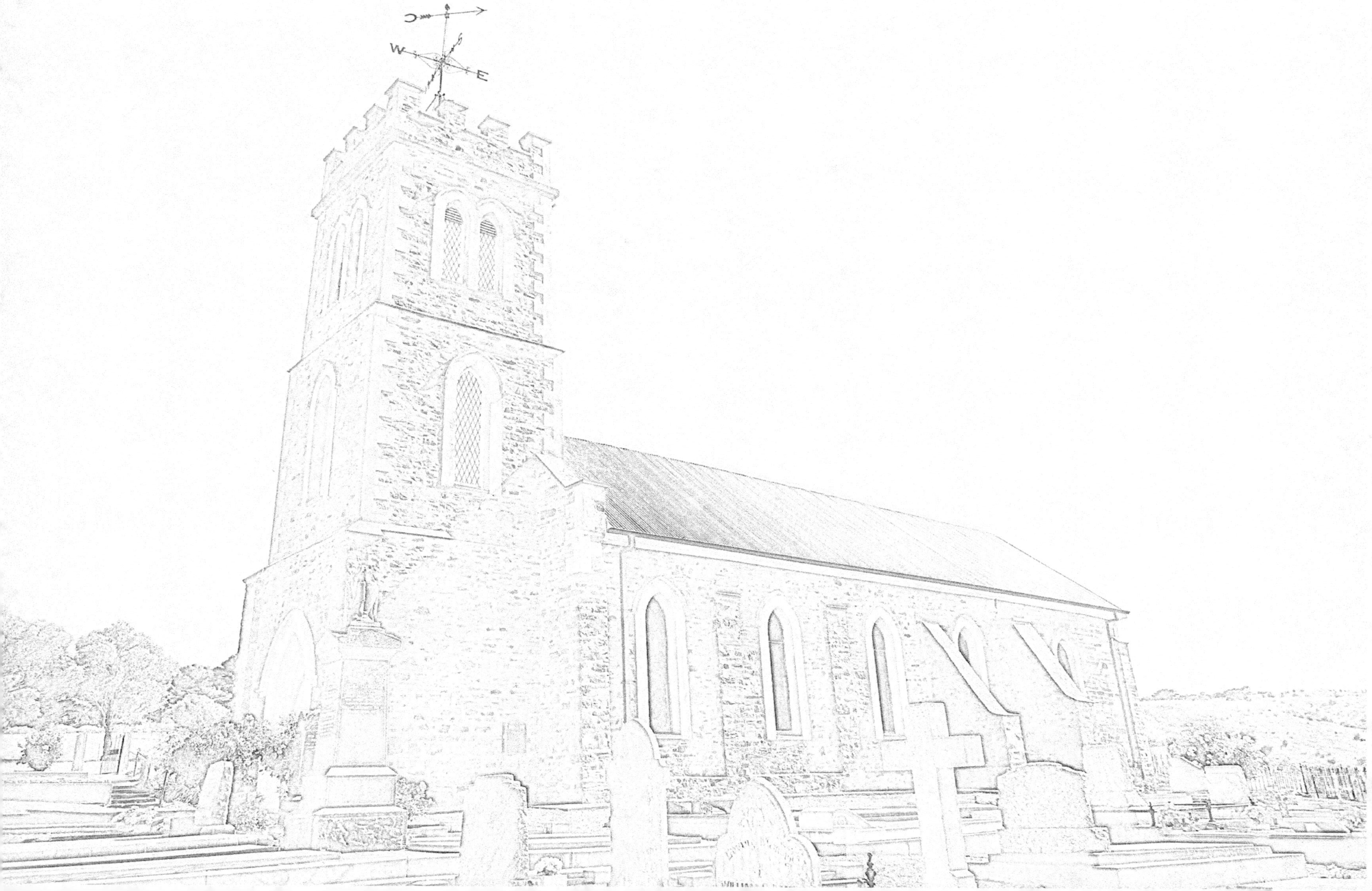
W
E

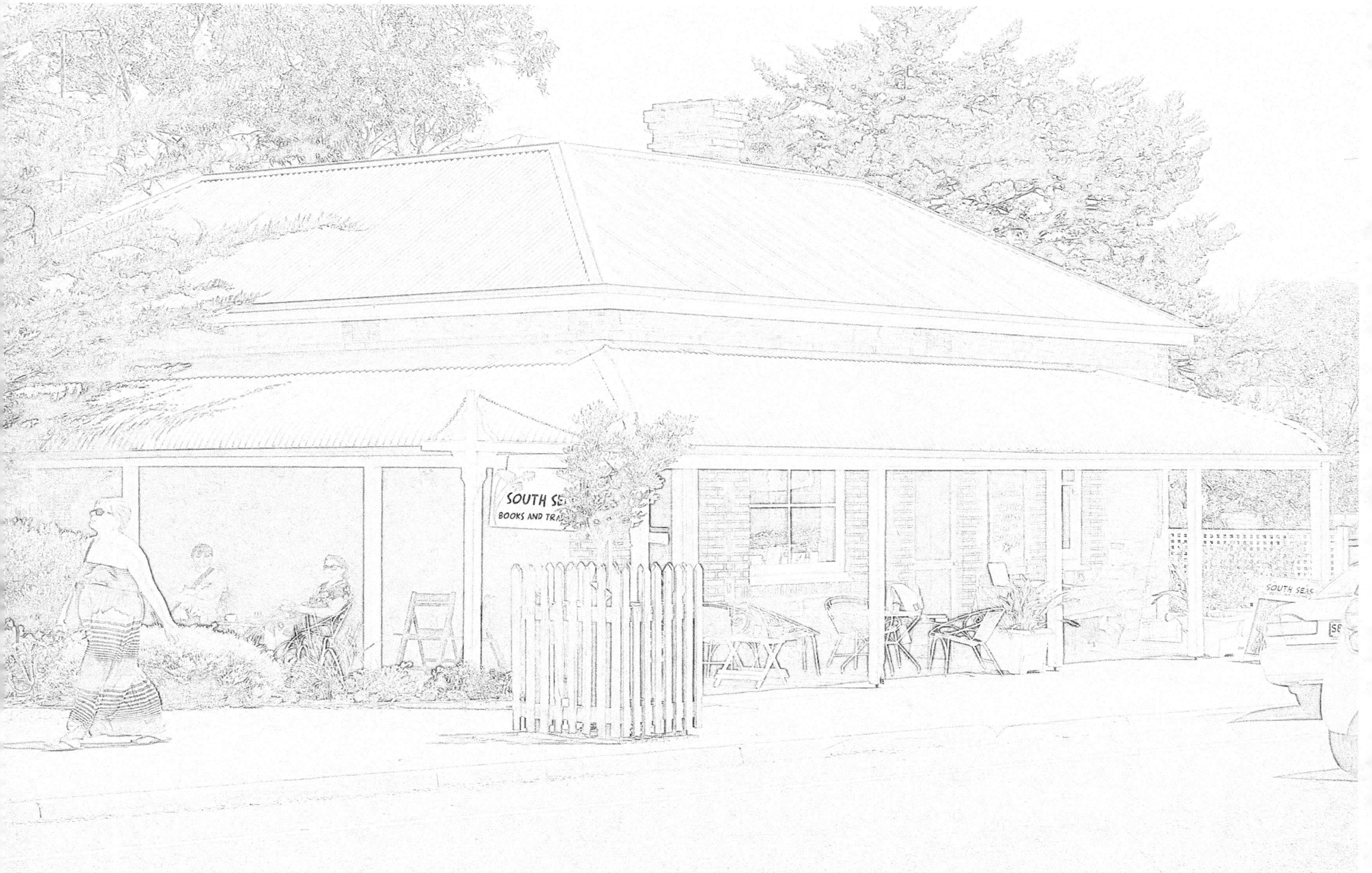
SOUTH SE
BOOKS AND TRA
SOUTH SEAS

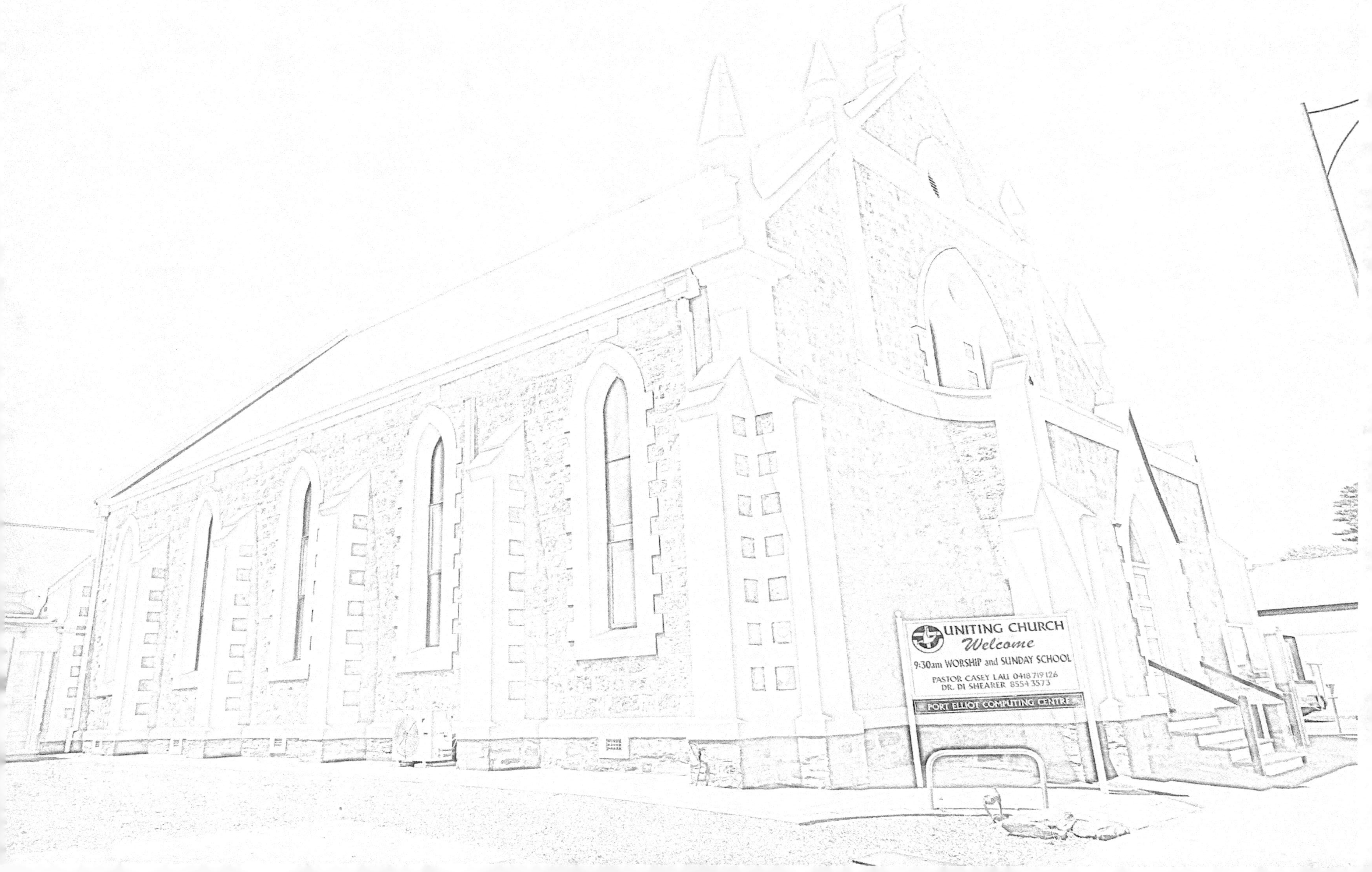
UNITING CHURCH
Welcome
9:30am WORSHIP and SUNDAY SCHOOL
PASTOR CASEY LAU 0418 719 126
DR. DI SHEARER 8554 3573
PORT ELLIOT COMPUTING CENTRE

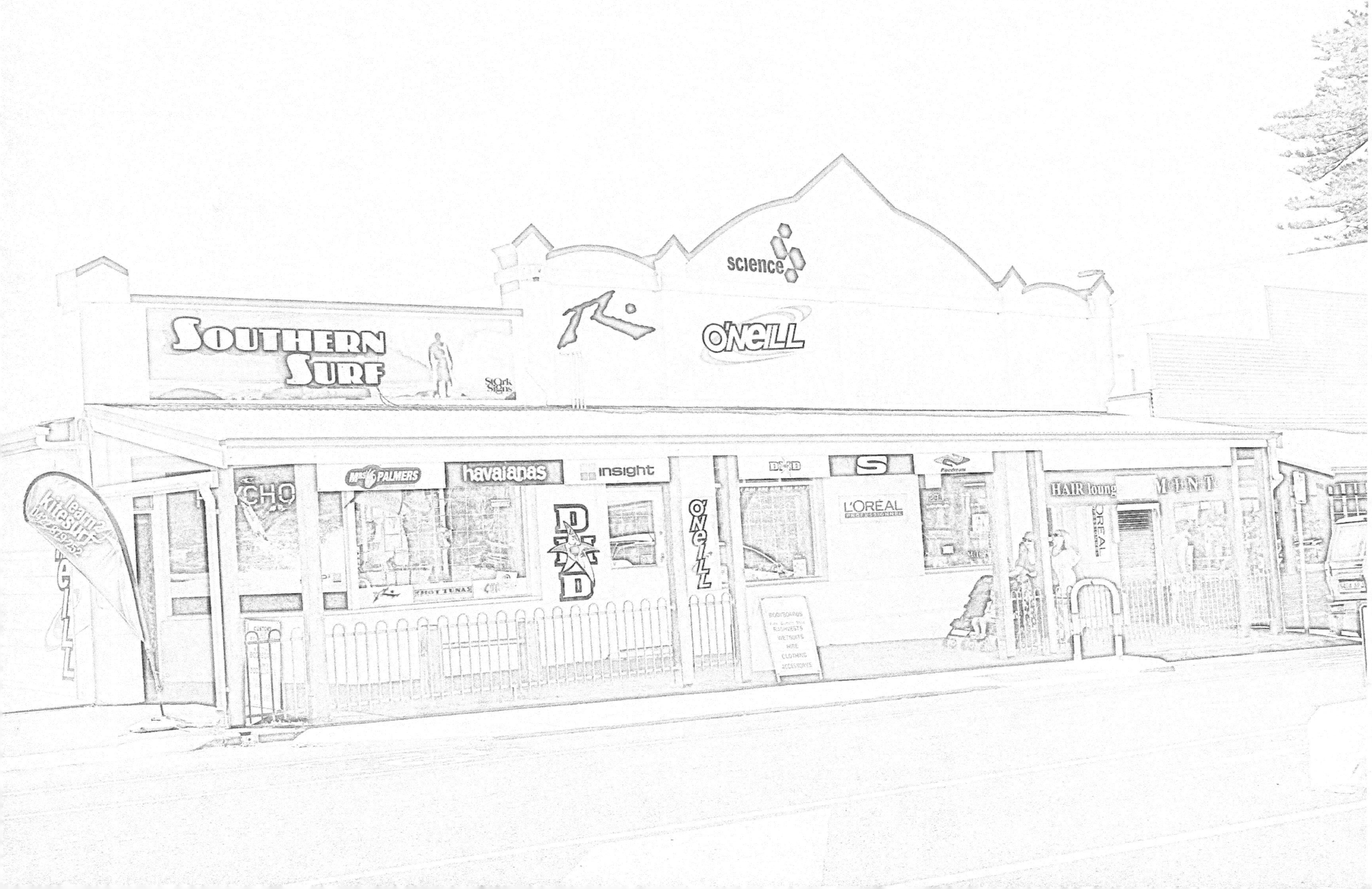
science
SOUTHERN SURF
O'NEILL
havaianas
insight
L'ORÉAL
HAIR lounge
O'NEILL

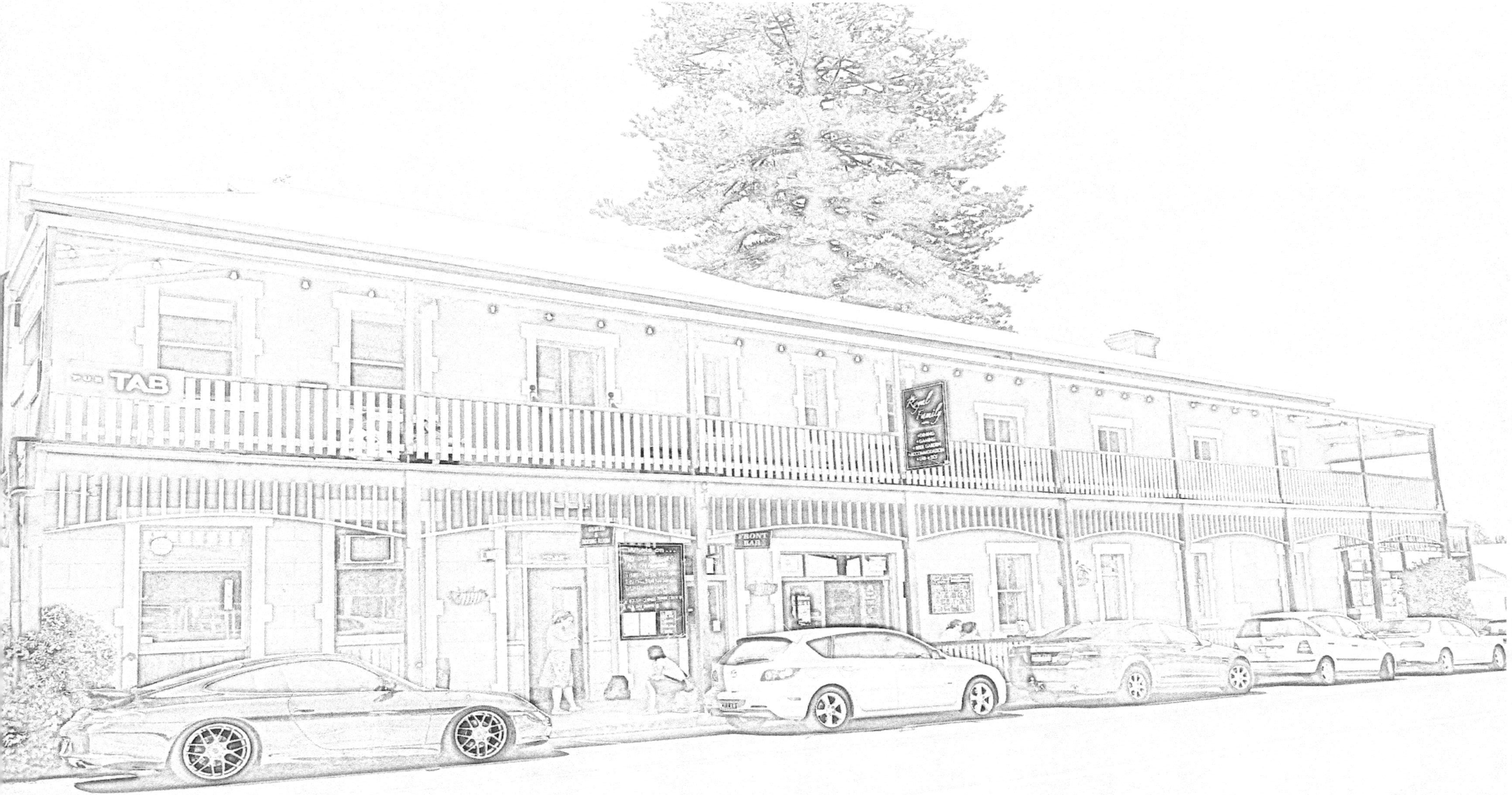
TAB
FRONT BAR

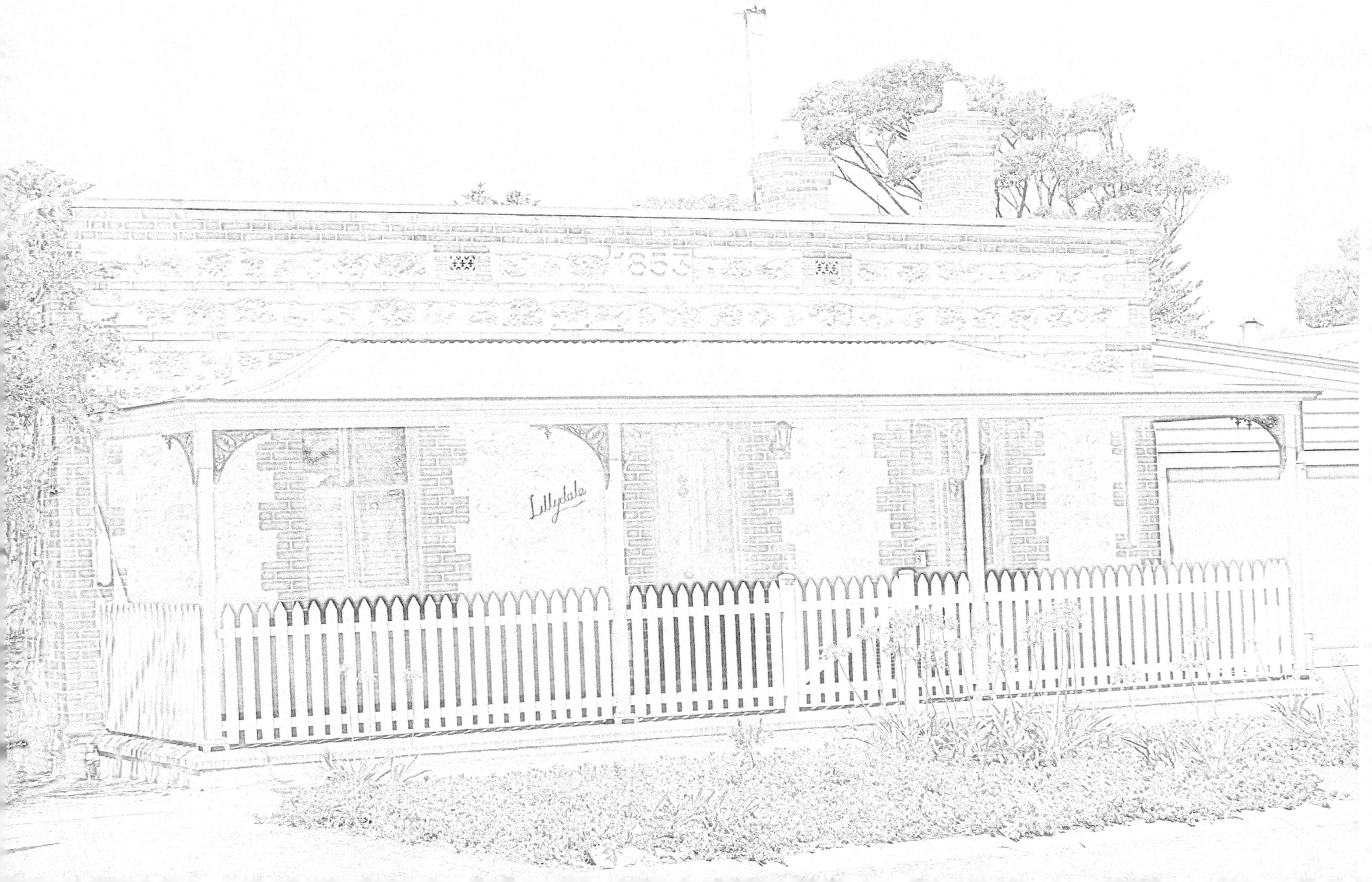
1853
Lillydale

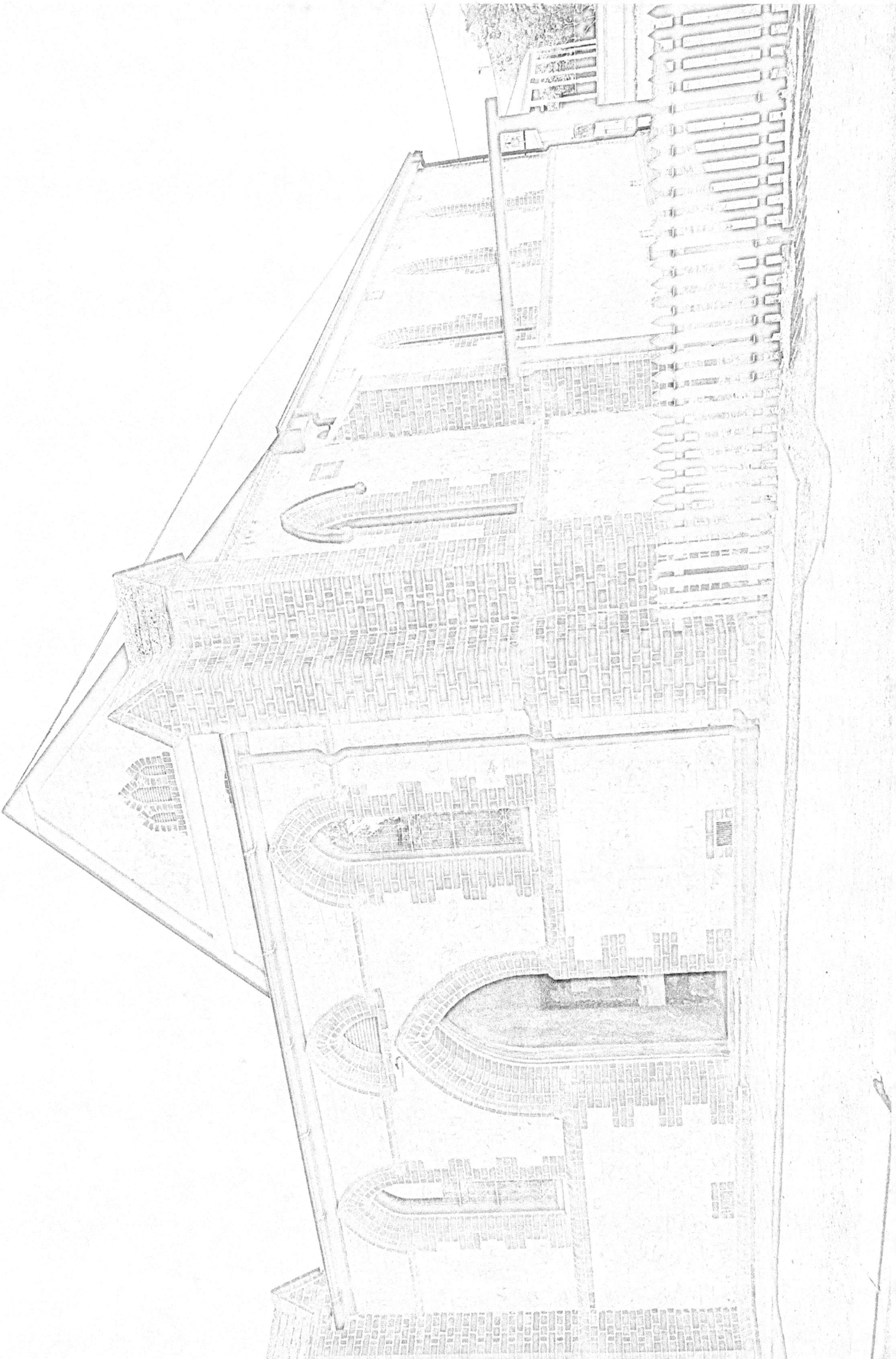

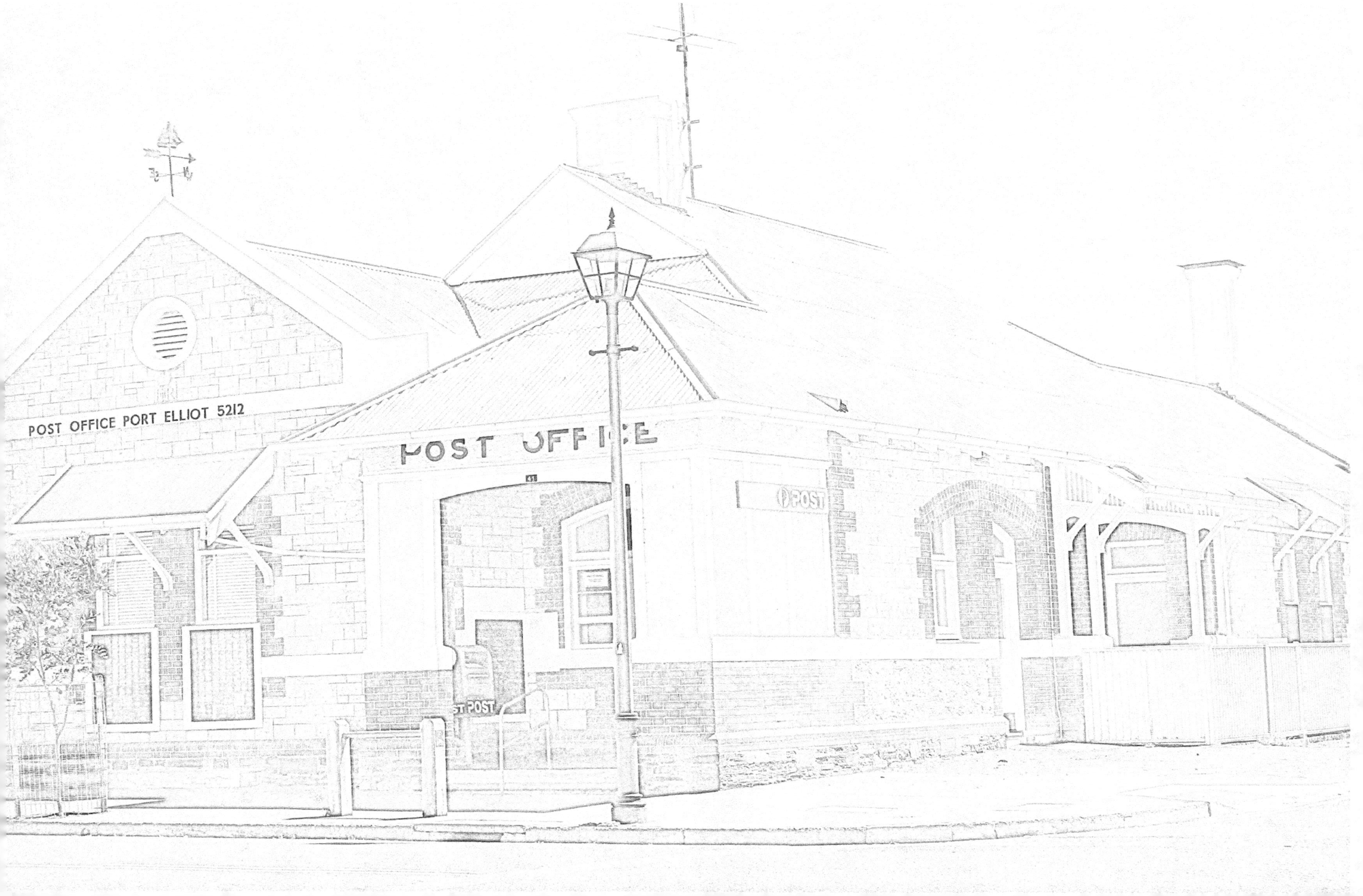
POST OFFICE PORT ELLIOT 5212
POST OFFICE
POST

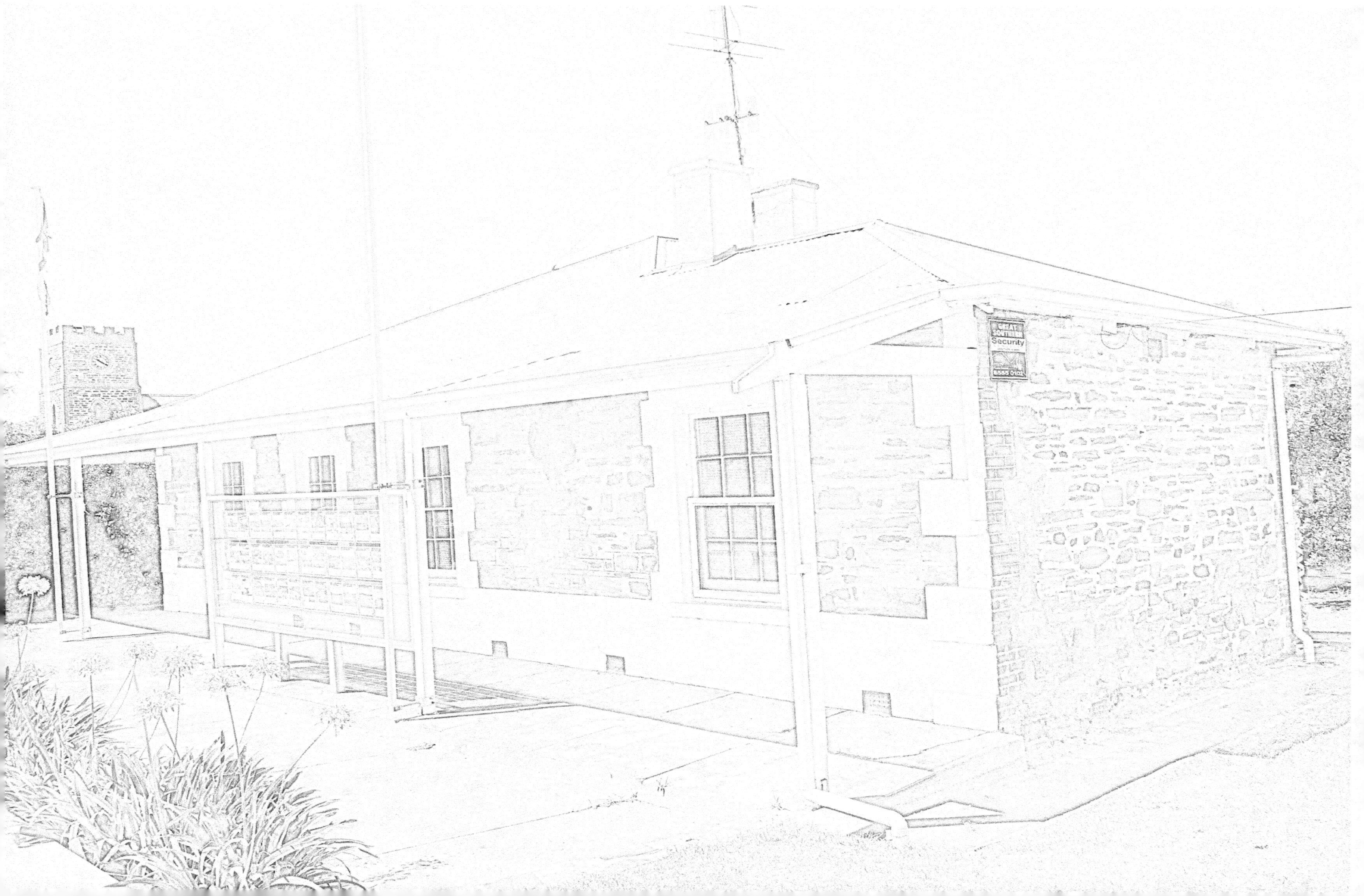
Security

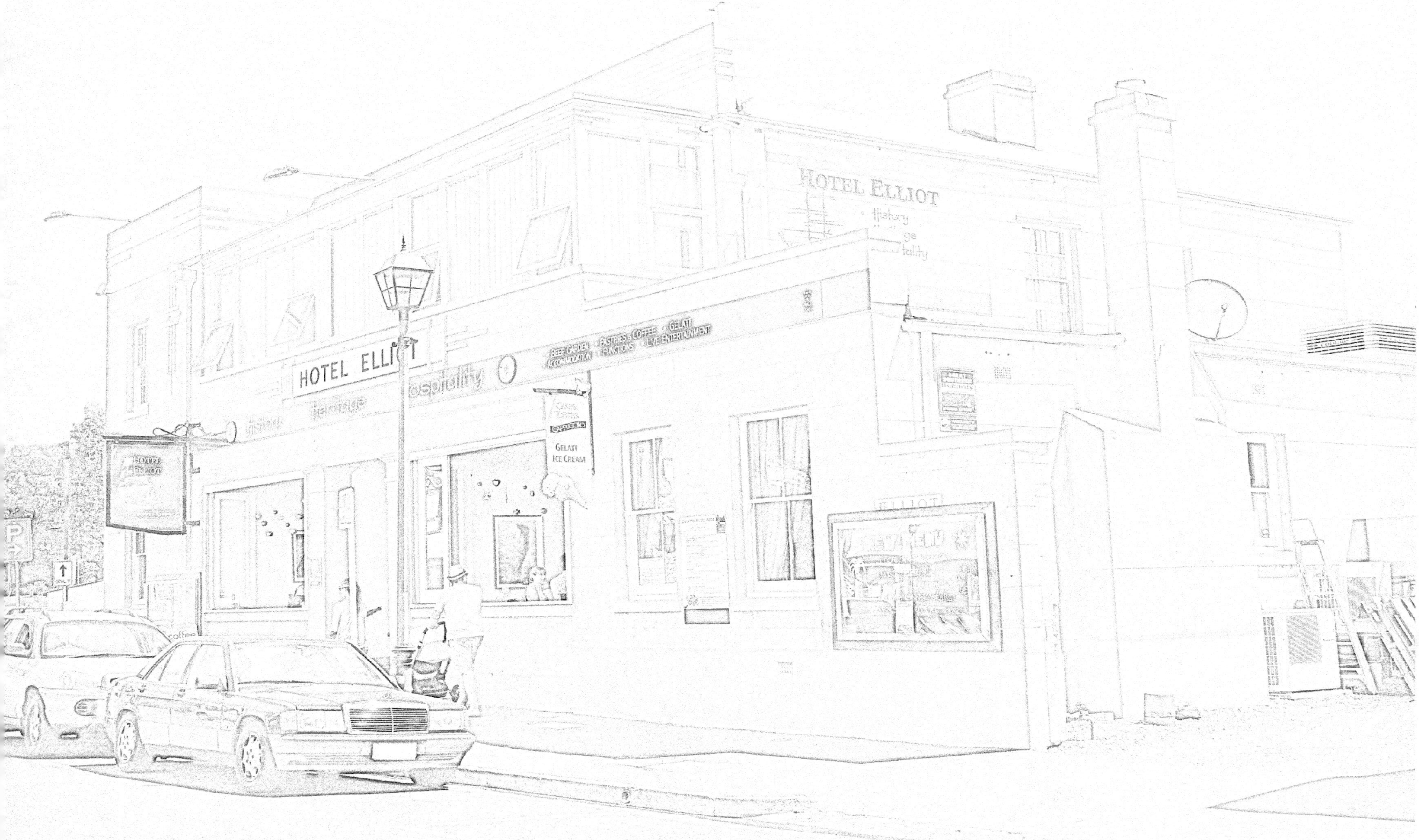
HOTEL ELLIOT
History
HOTEL ELLIOT
Heritage
ospitality
• BEER GARDEN • PASTRIES • COFFEE • GELATI
• ACCOMMODATION • FUNCTIONS • LIVE ENTERTAINMENT
GELATI
ICE CREAM
HOTEL ELLIOT
ELLIOT
P

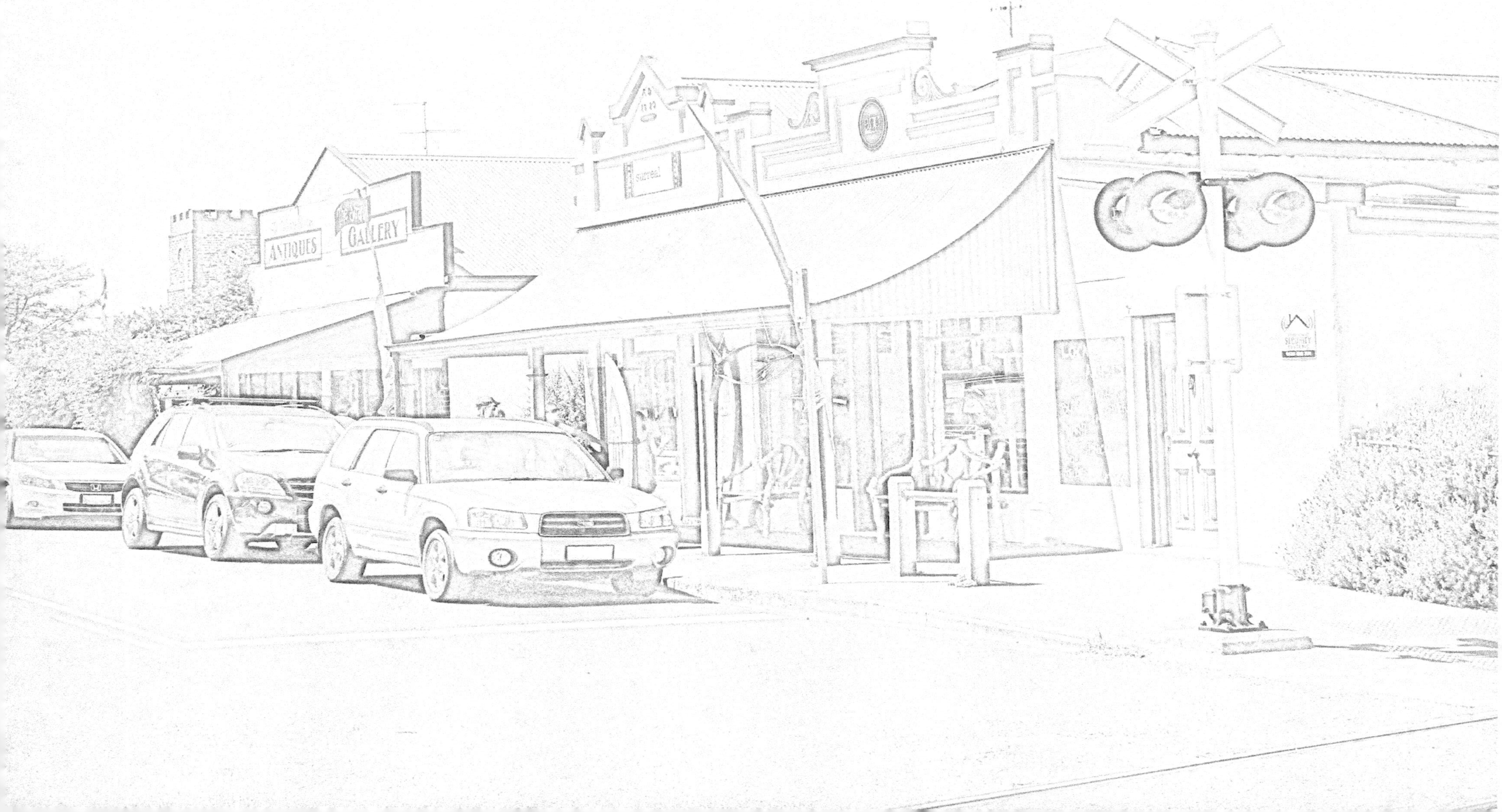
ANTIQUES
GALLERY

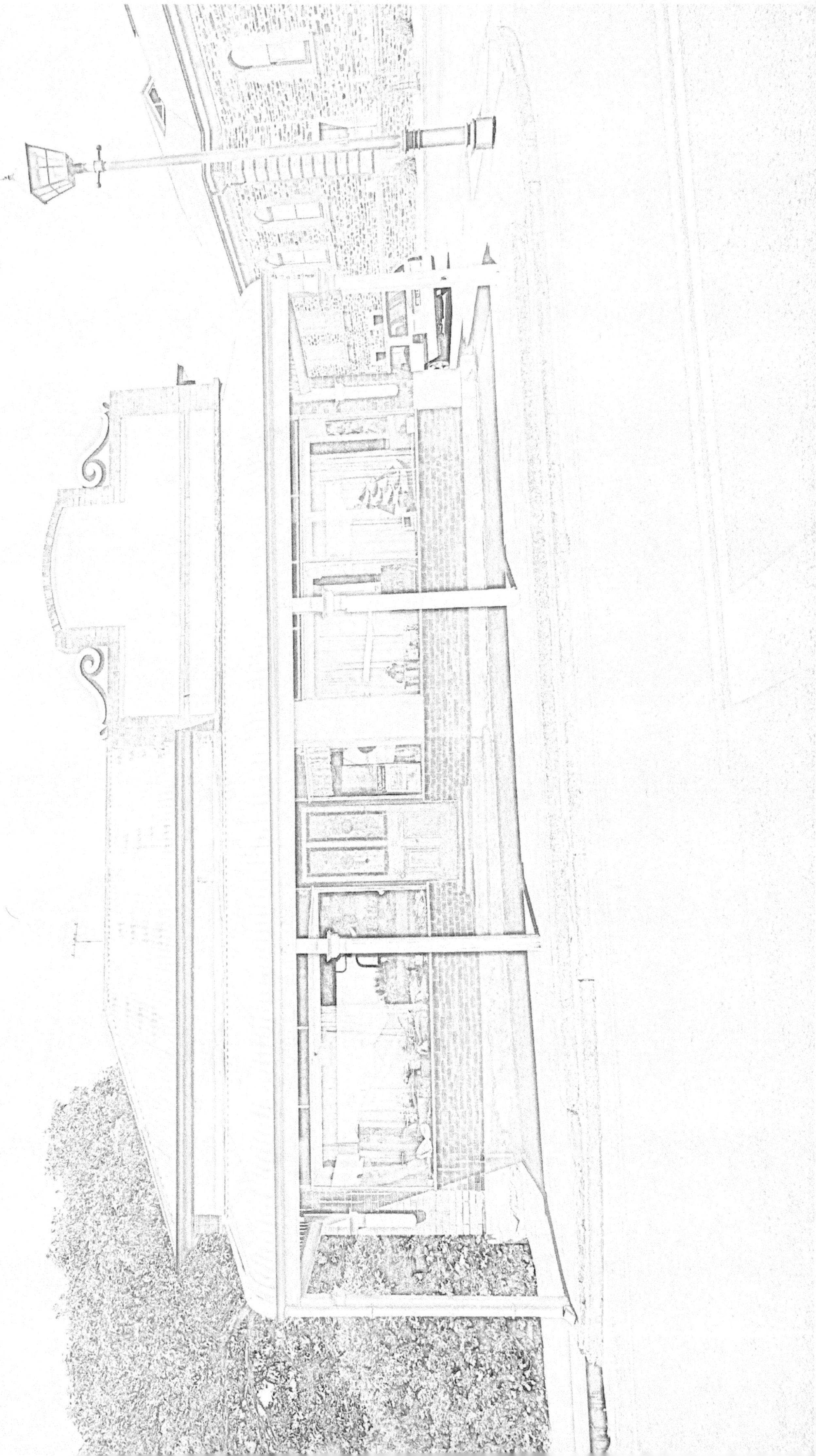

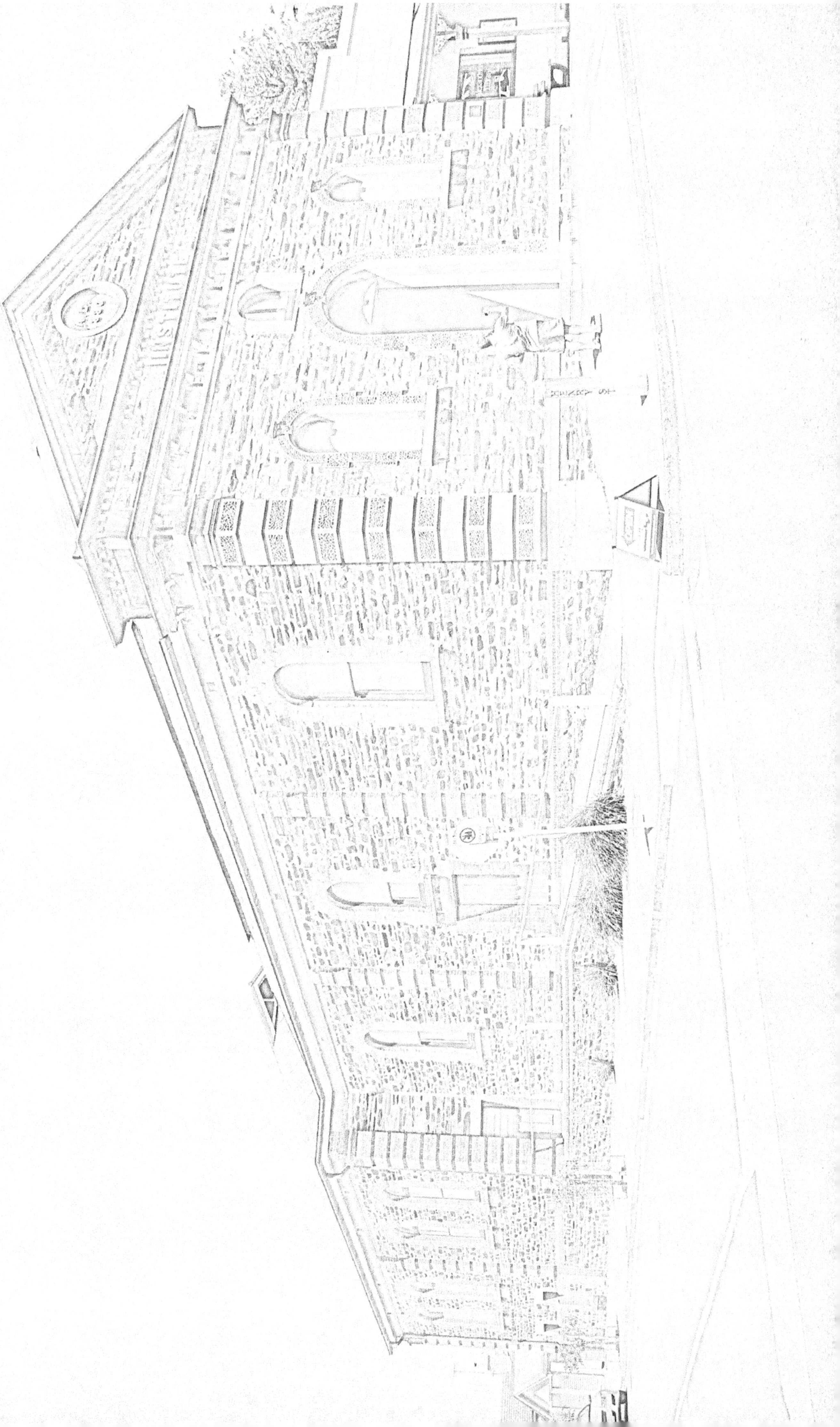

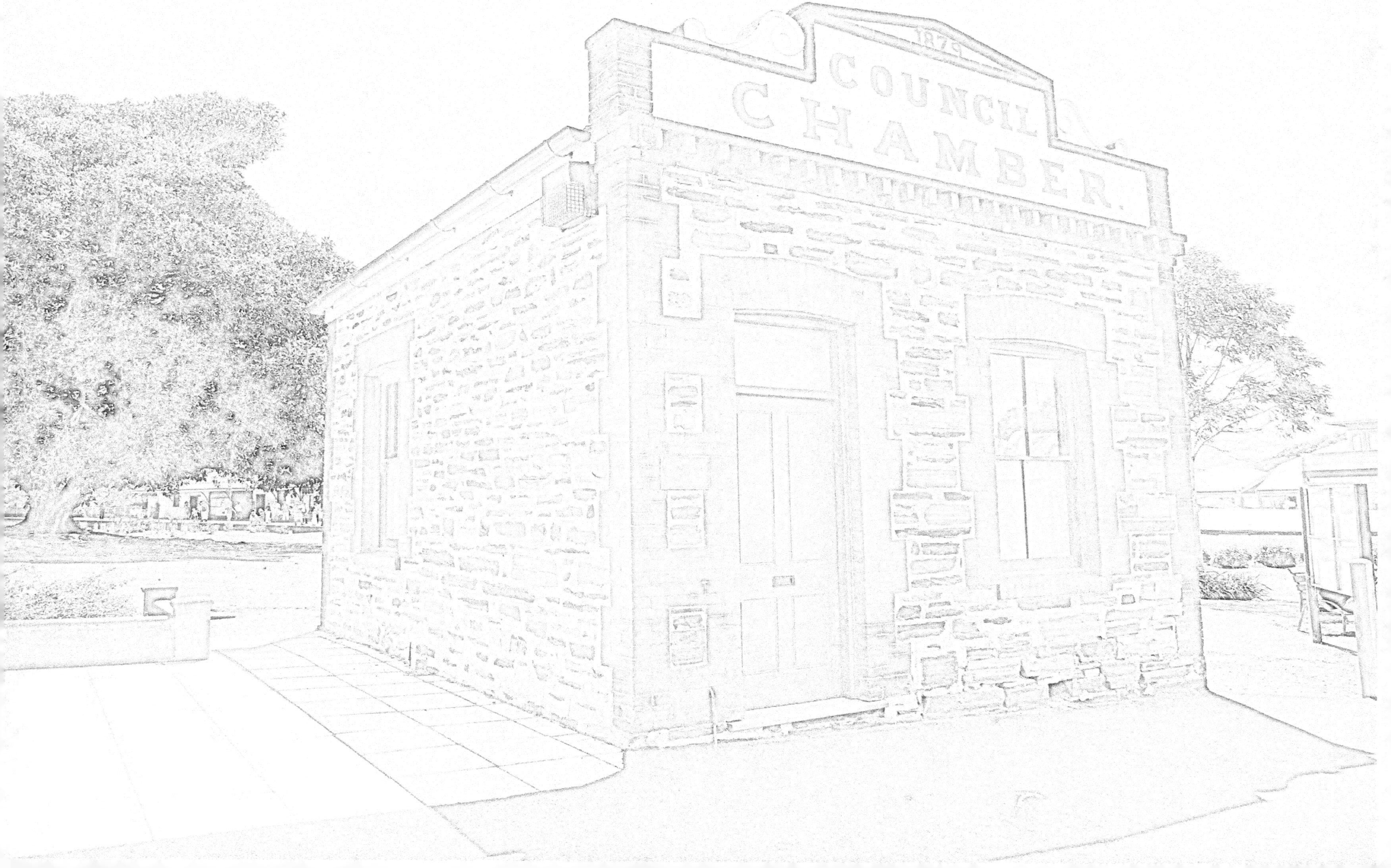
1879
COUNCIL
CHAMBER.

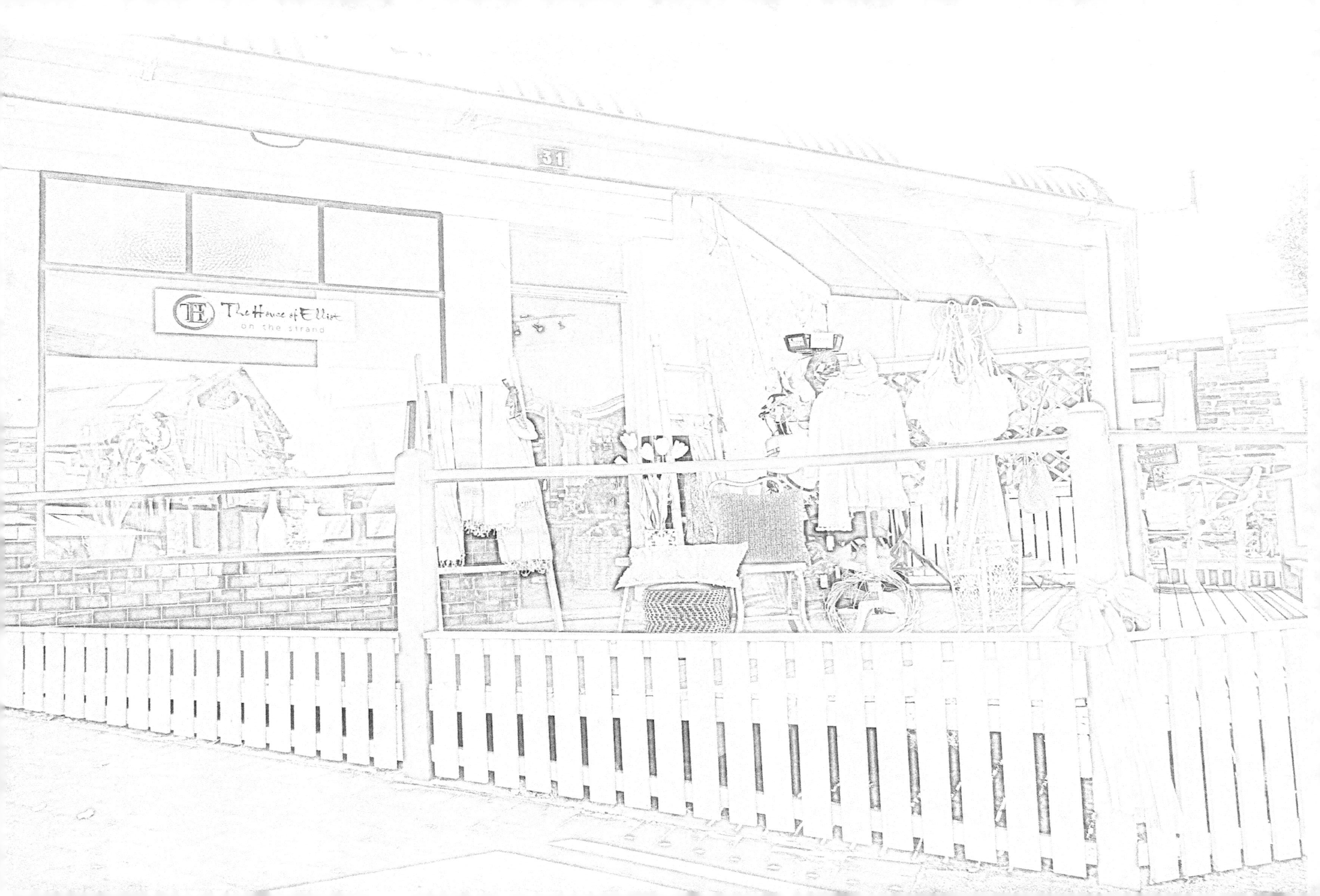
31
The House of Elliot
on the strand

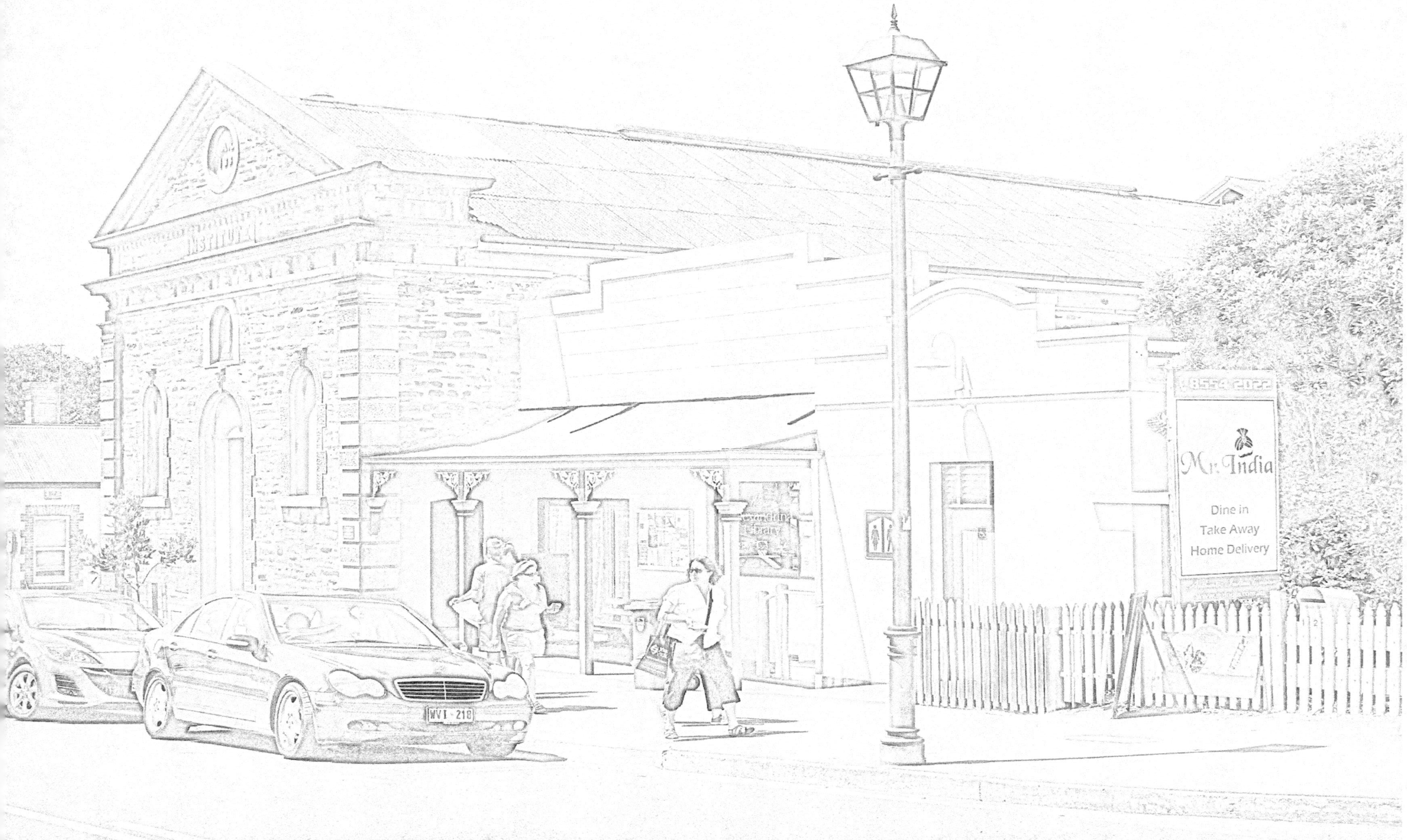

8554 2022
Mr. India
Dine in
Take Away
Home Delivery
WVI 218

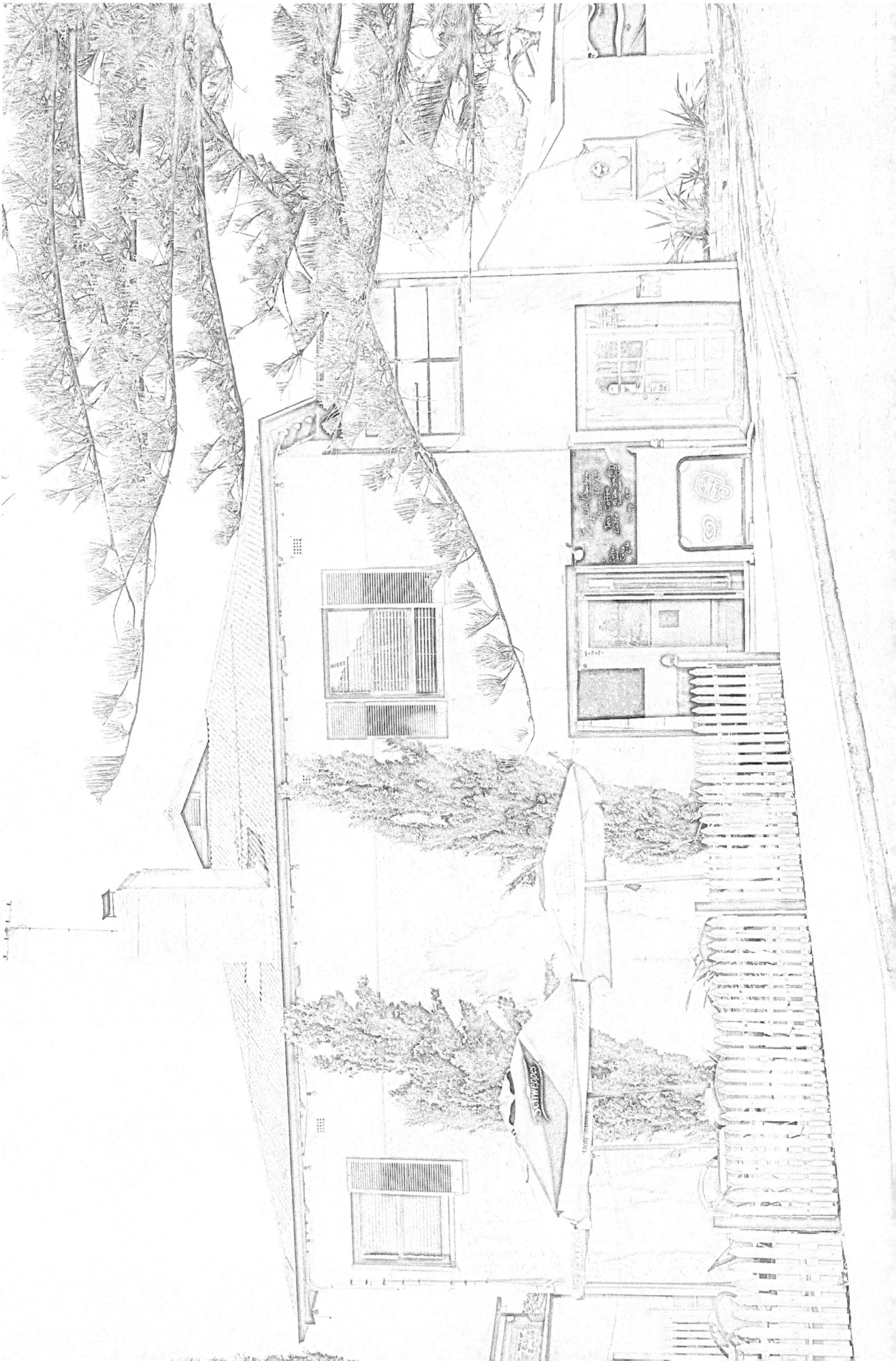

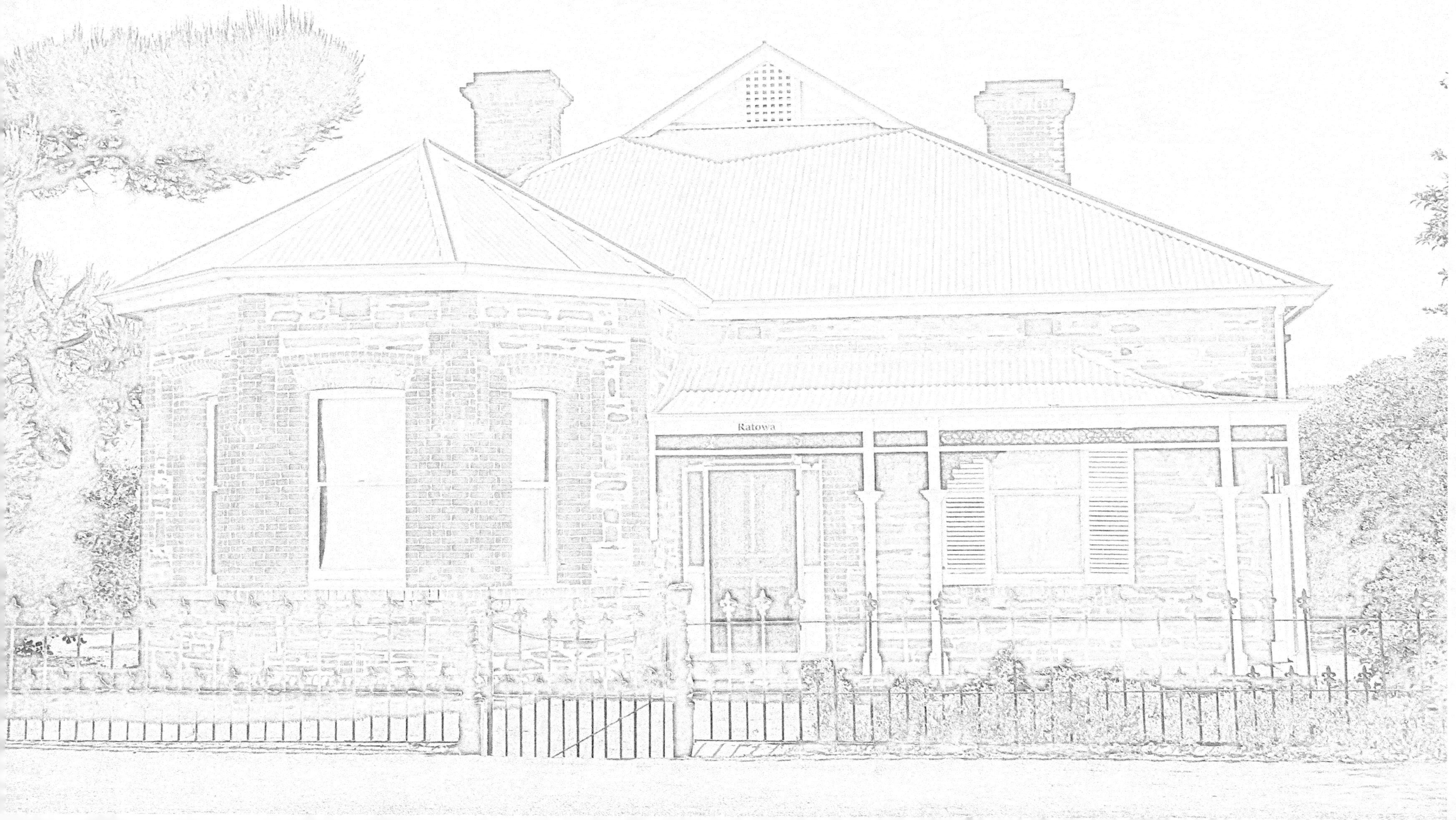
Ratowa

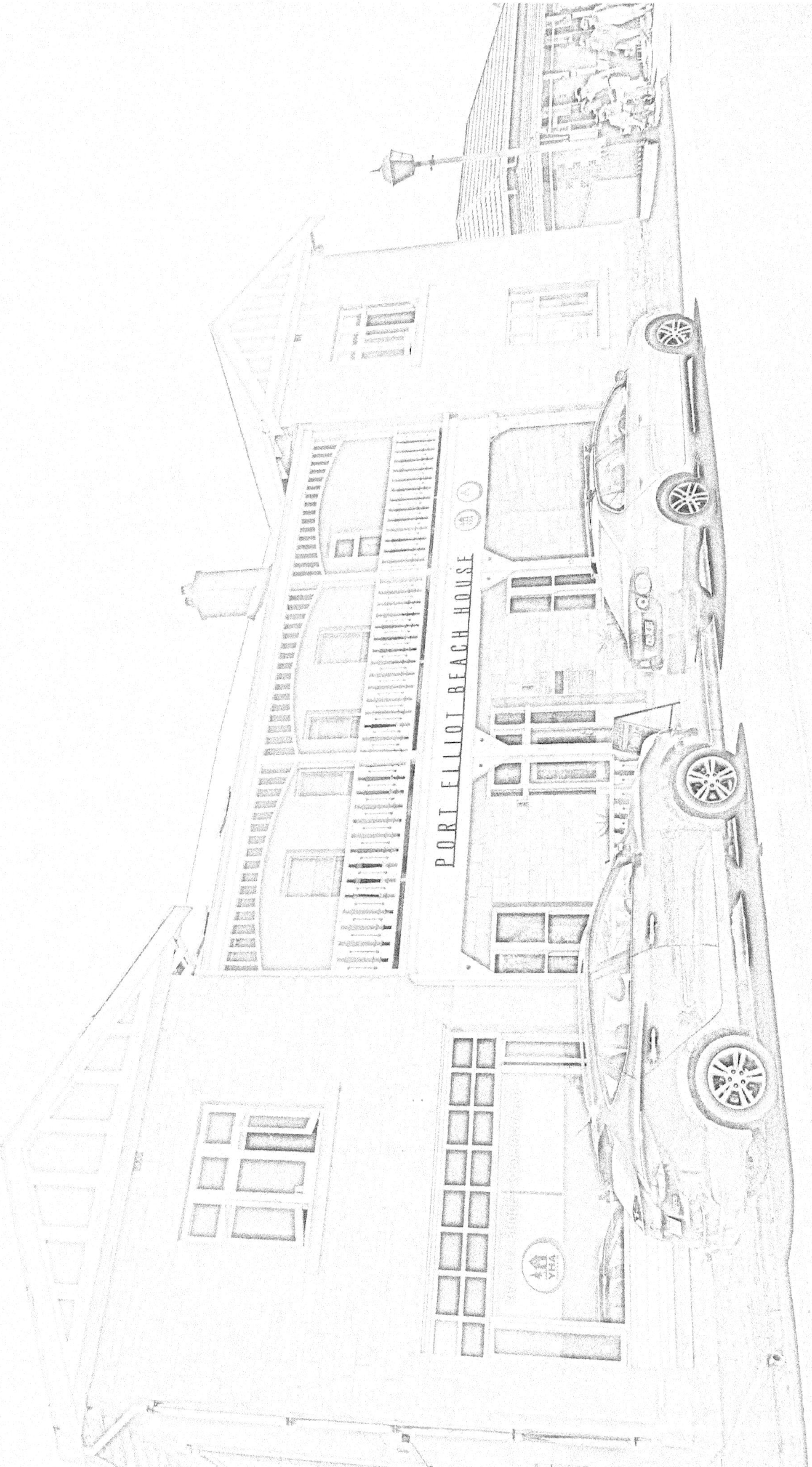
PORT ELLIOT BEACH HOUSE
YHA

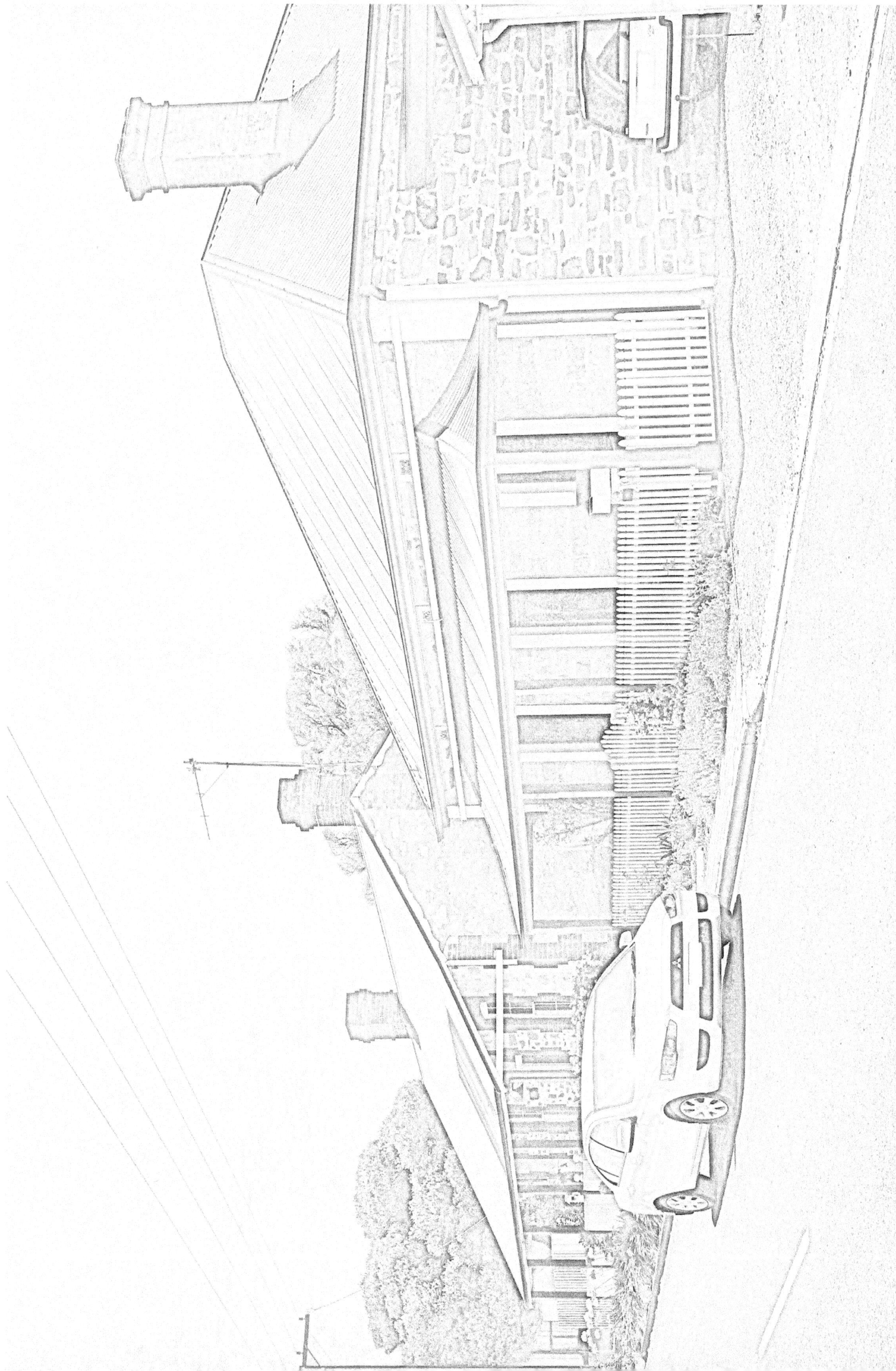

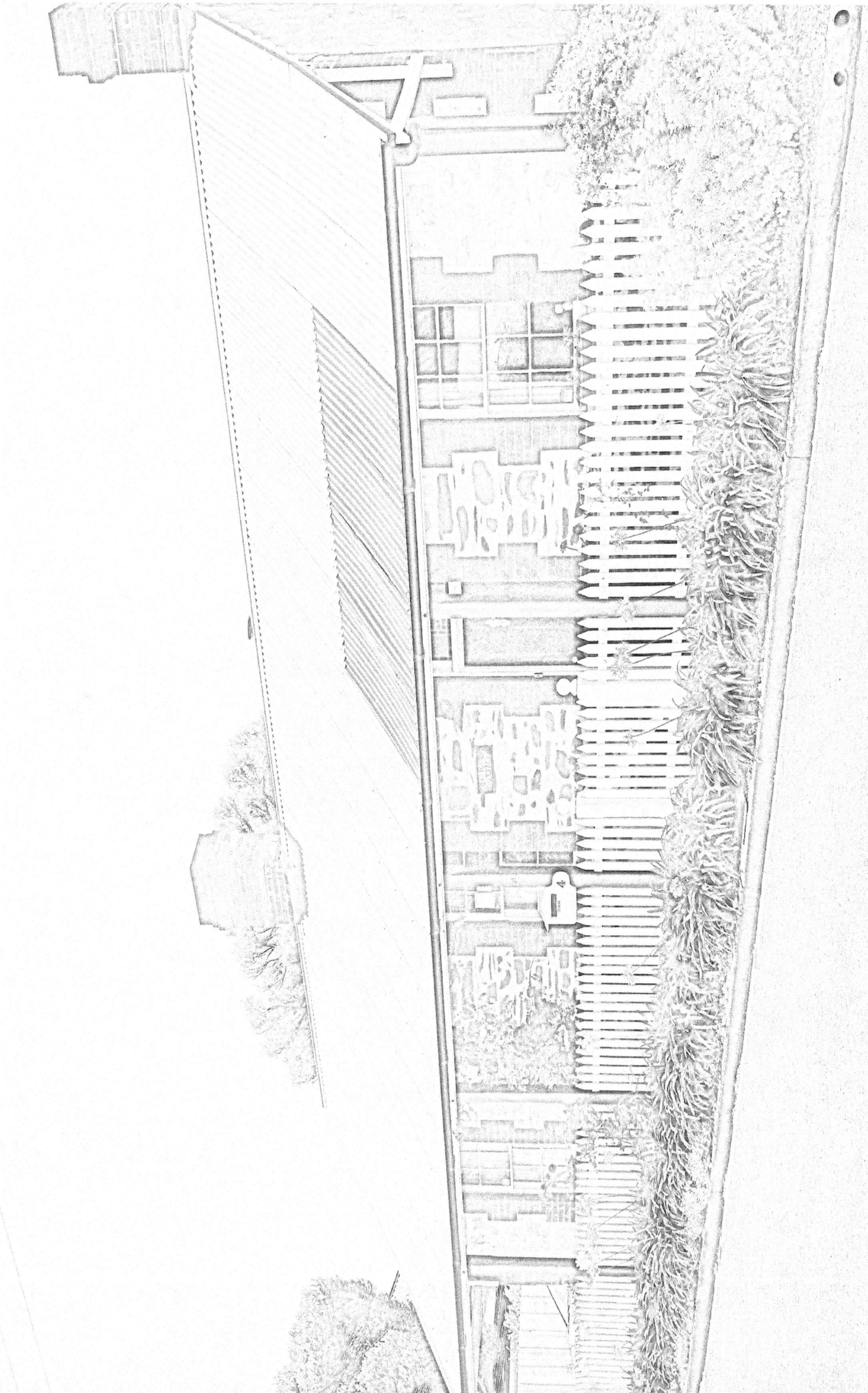

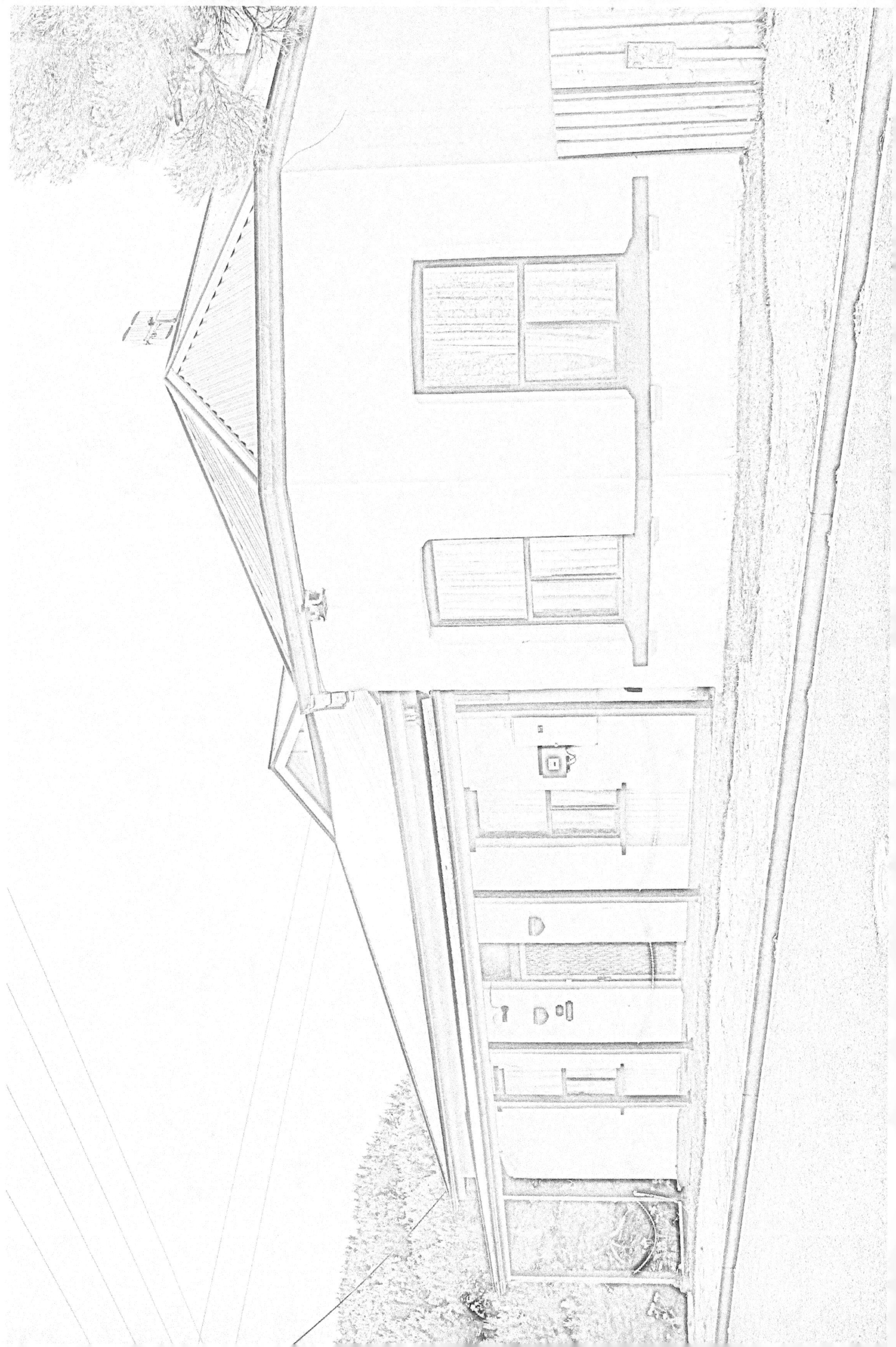

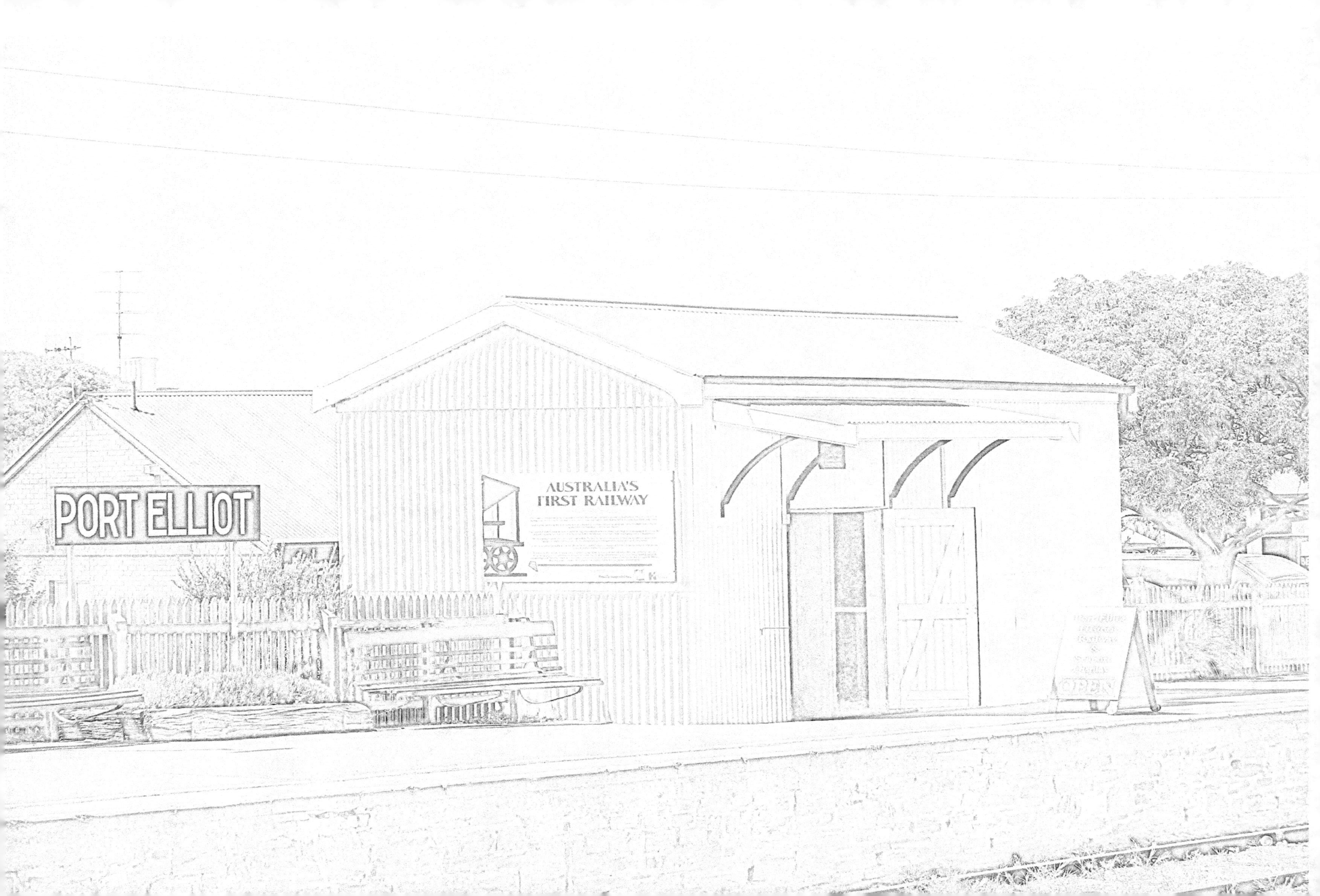
PORT ELLIOT
AUSTRALIA'S
FIRST RAILWAY
OPEN

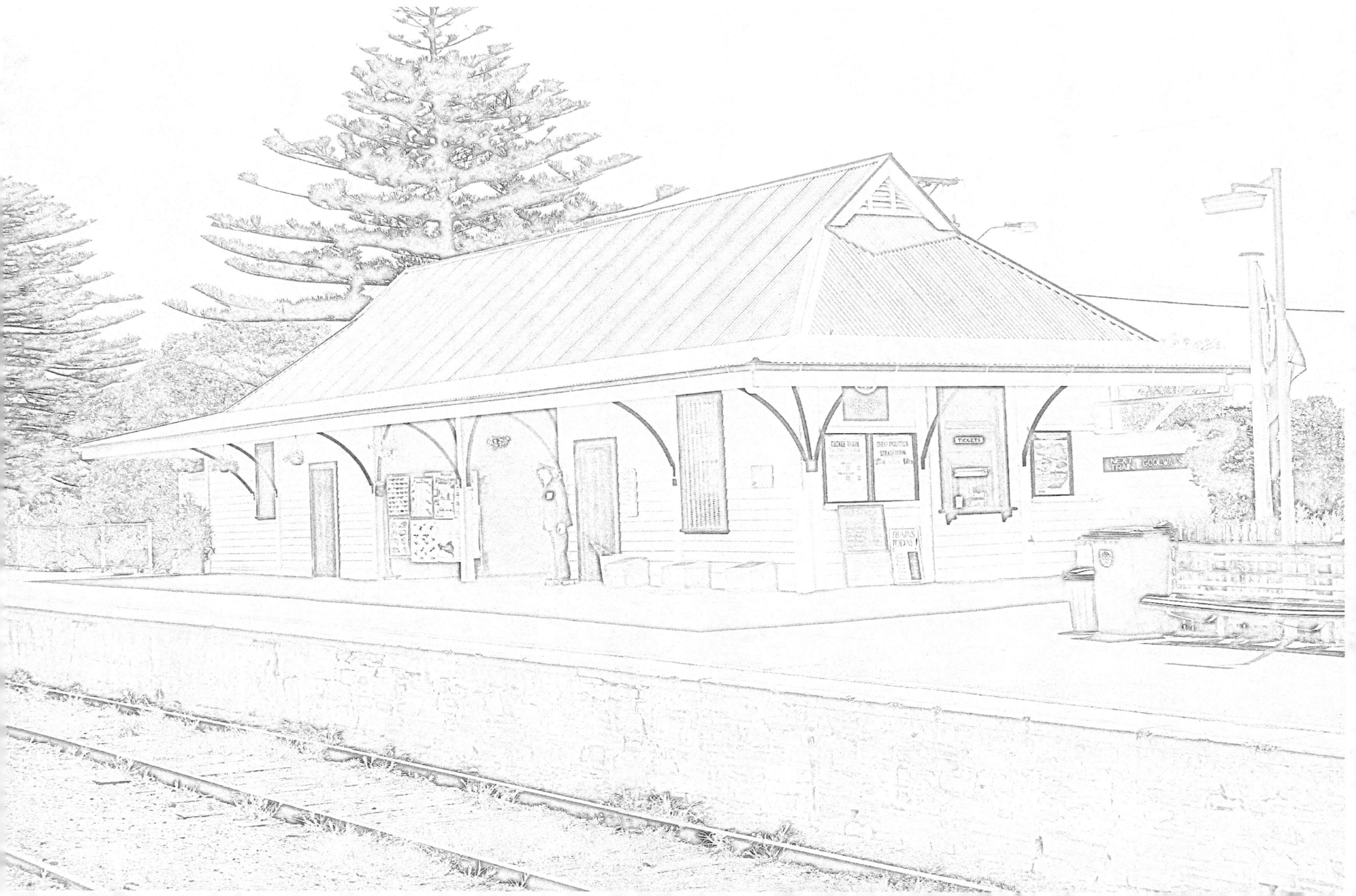

TICKETS
NEXT TRAIN GOOLWA
COCKLE TRAIN
TRAINS TODAY

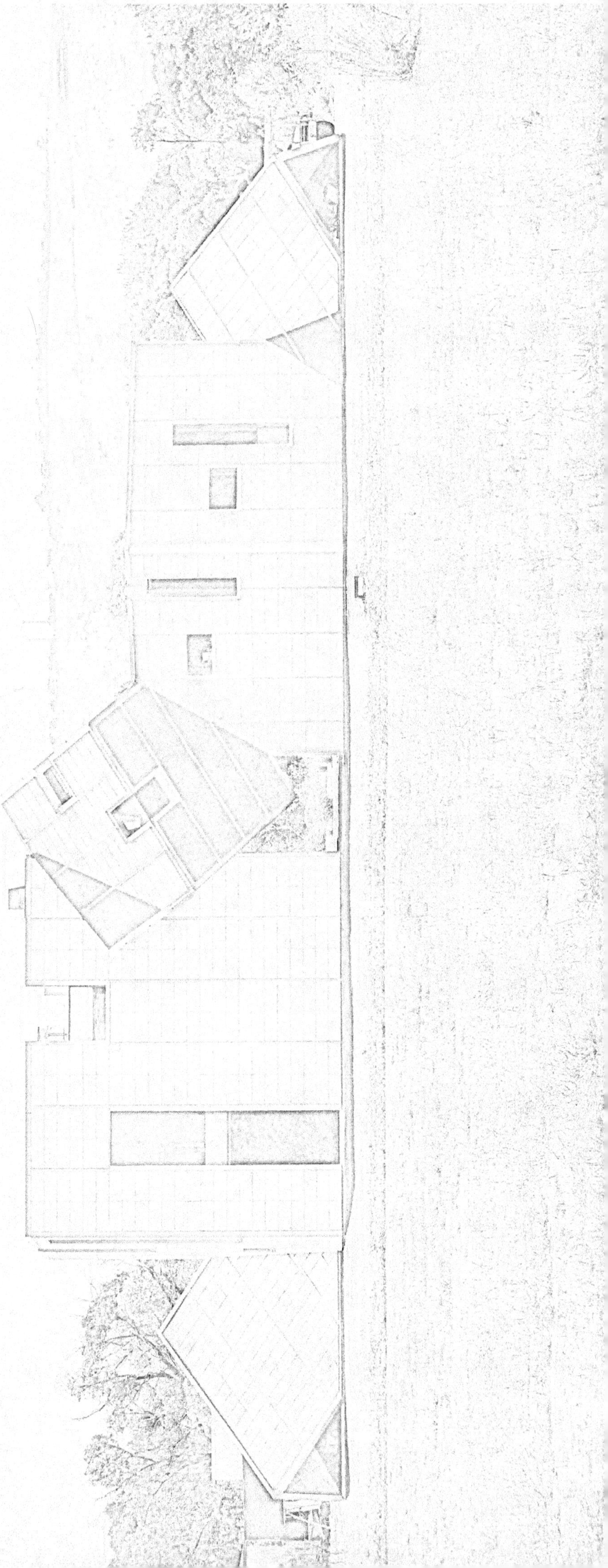

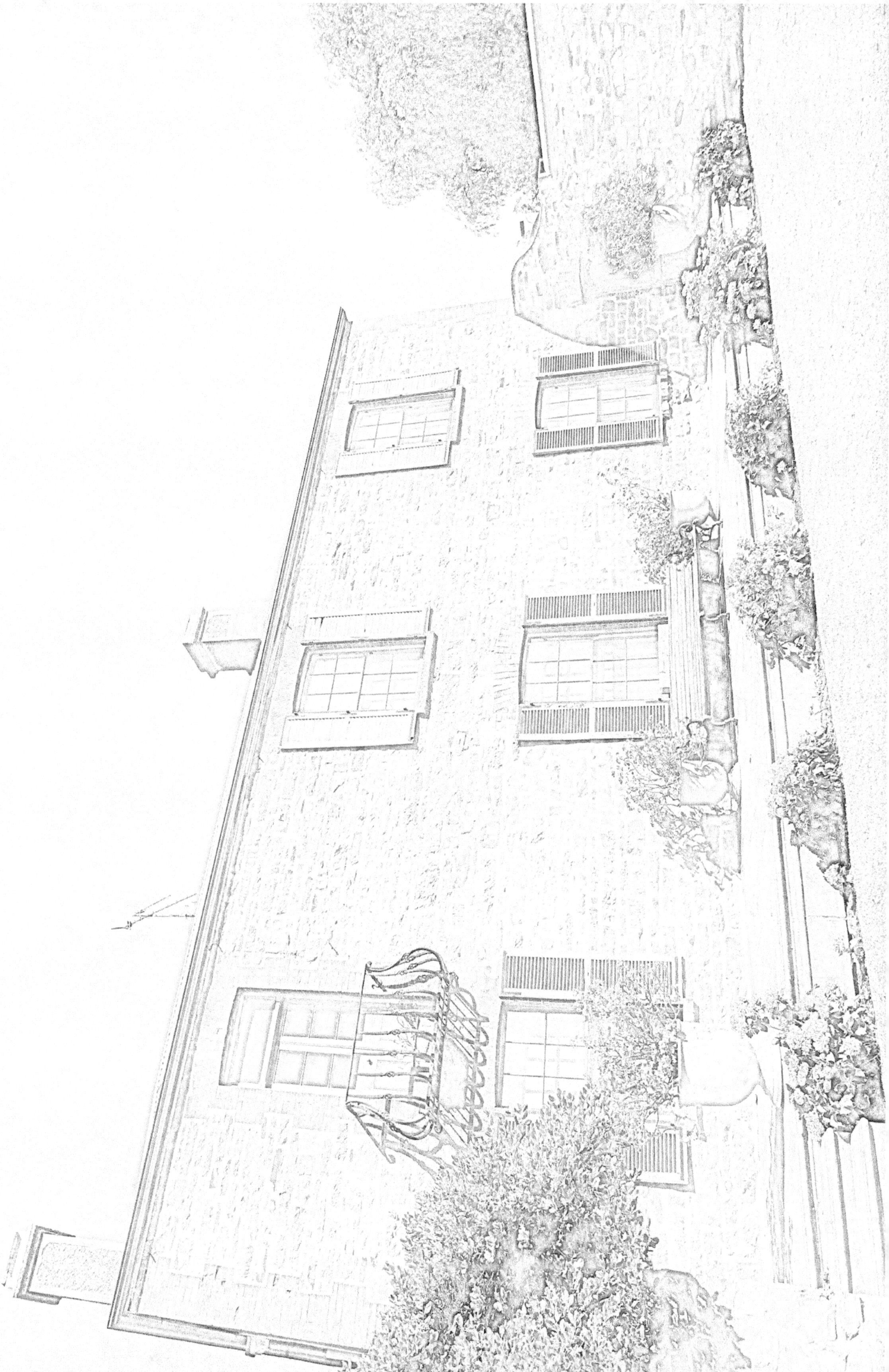

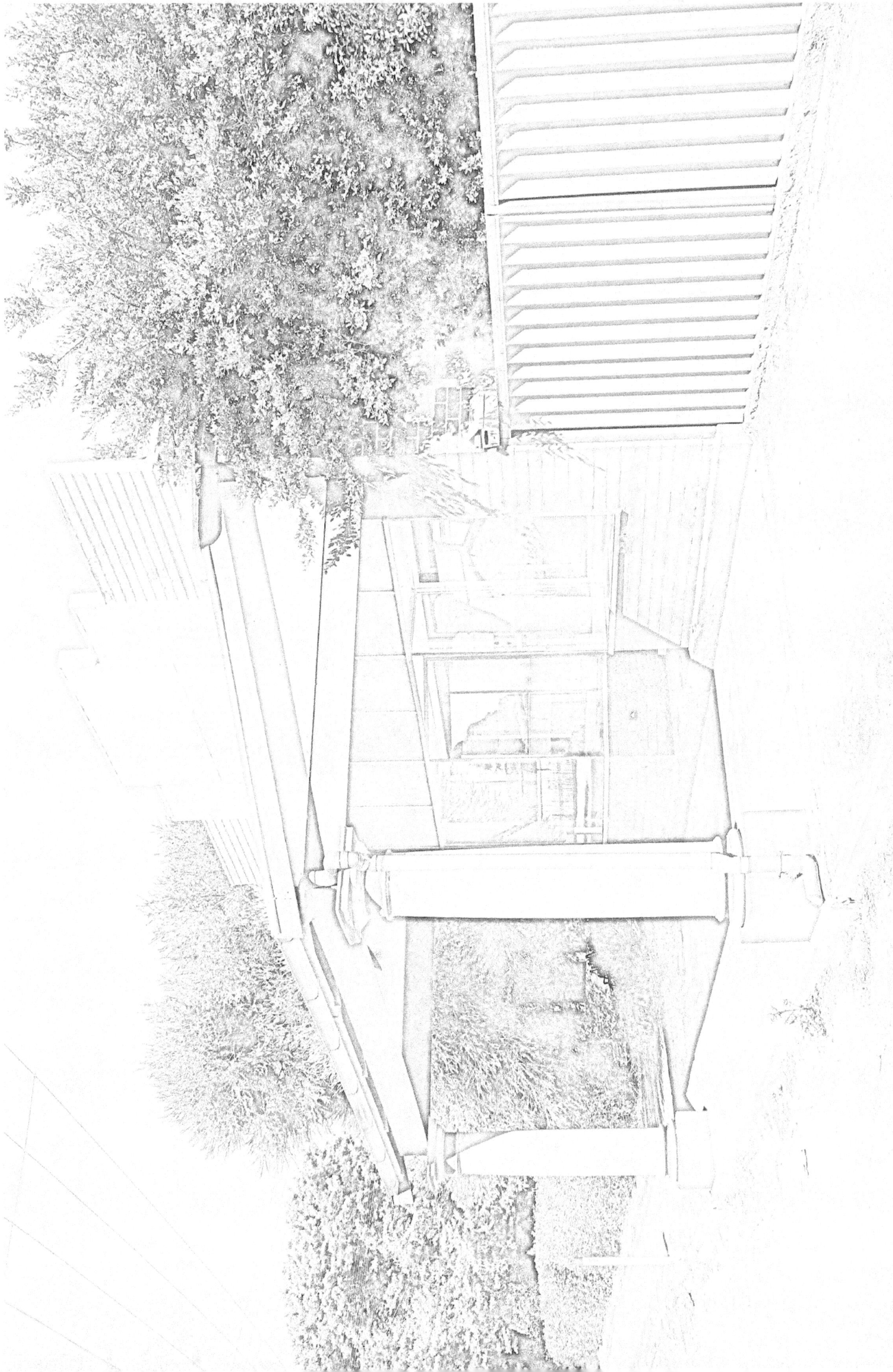

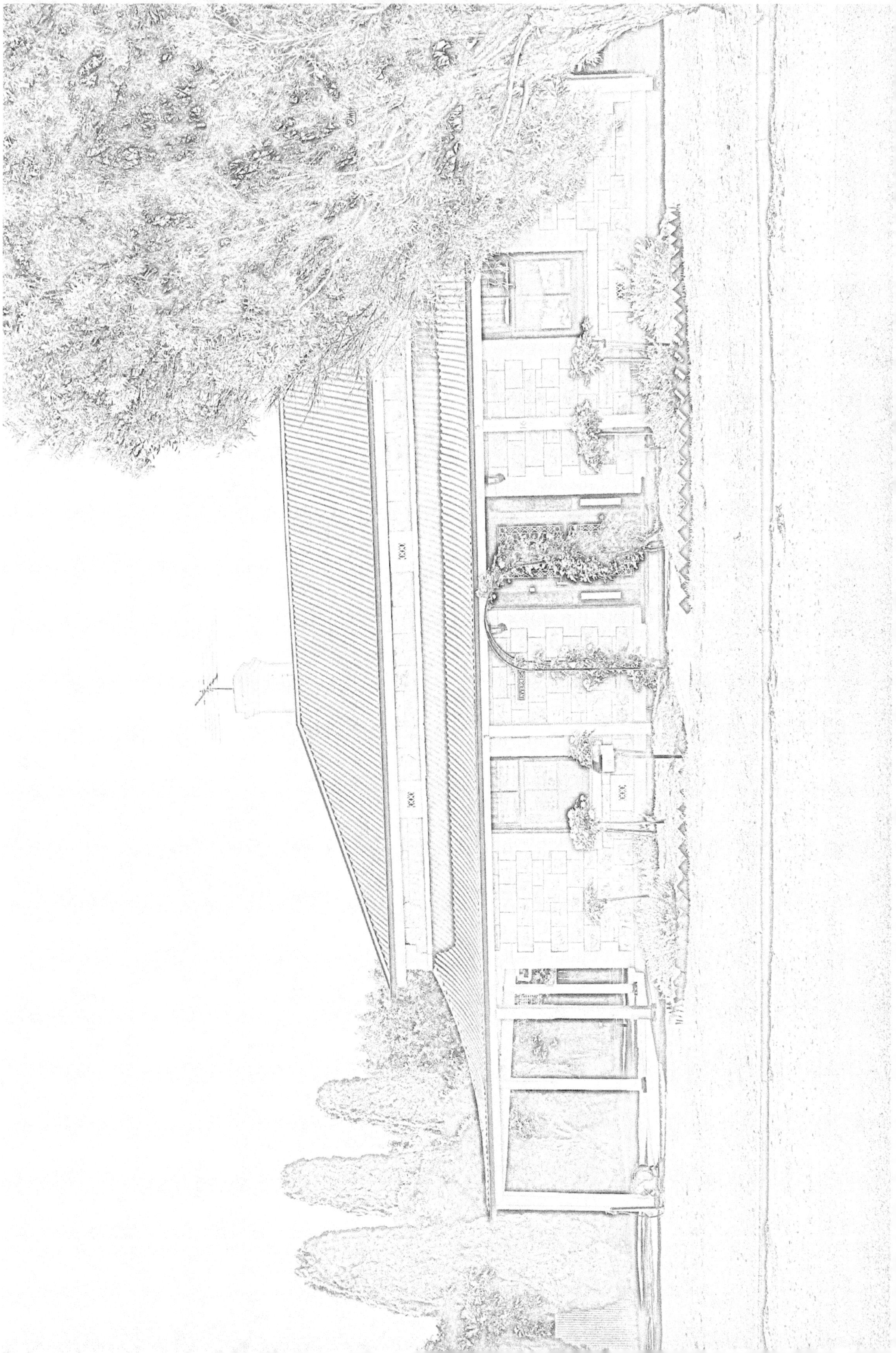

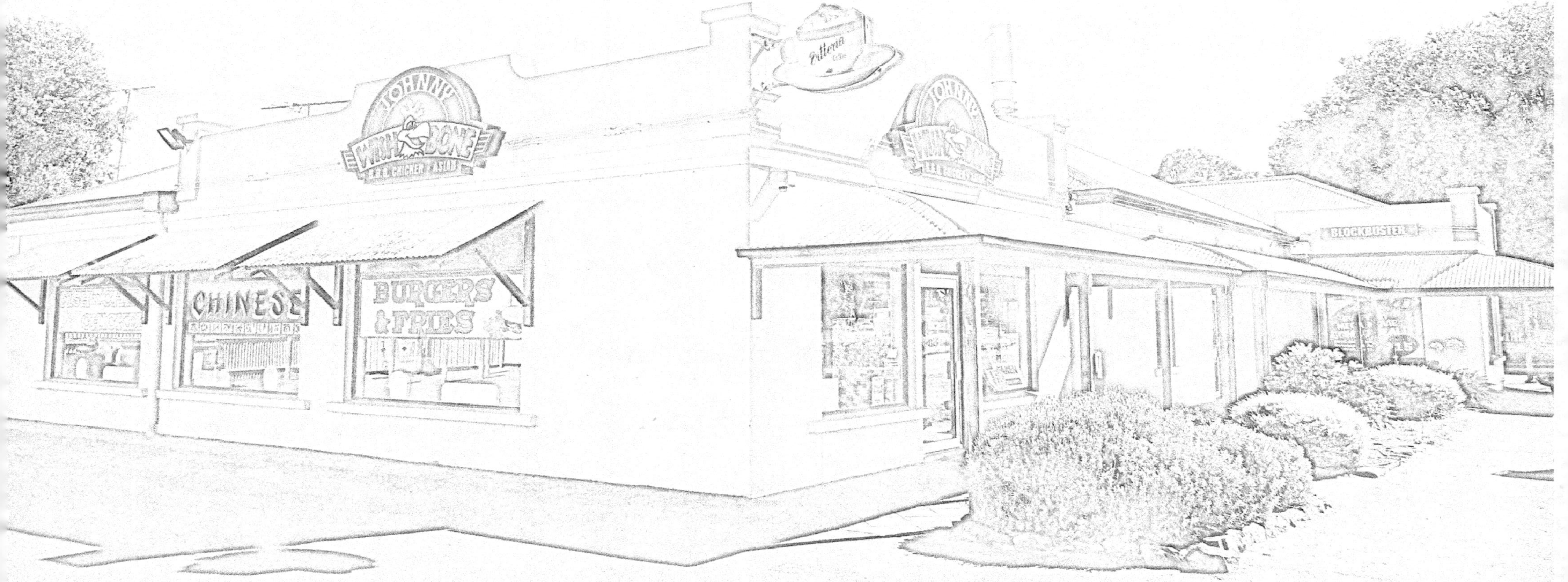
JOHNNY
WISH BONE
CHINESE
BURGERS & FRIES
BLOCKBUSTER

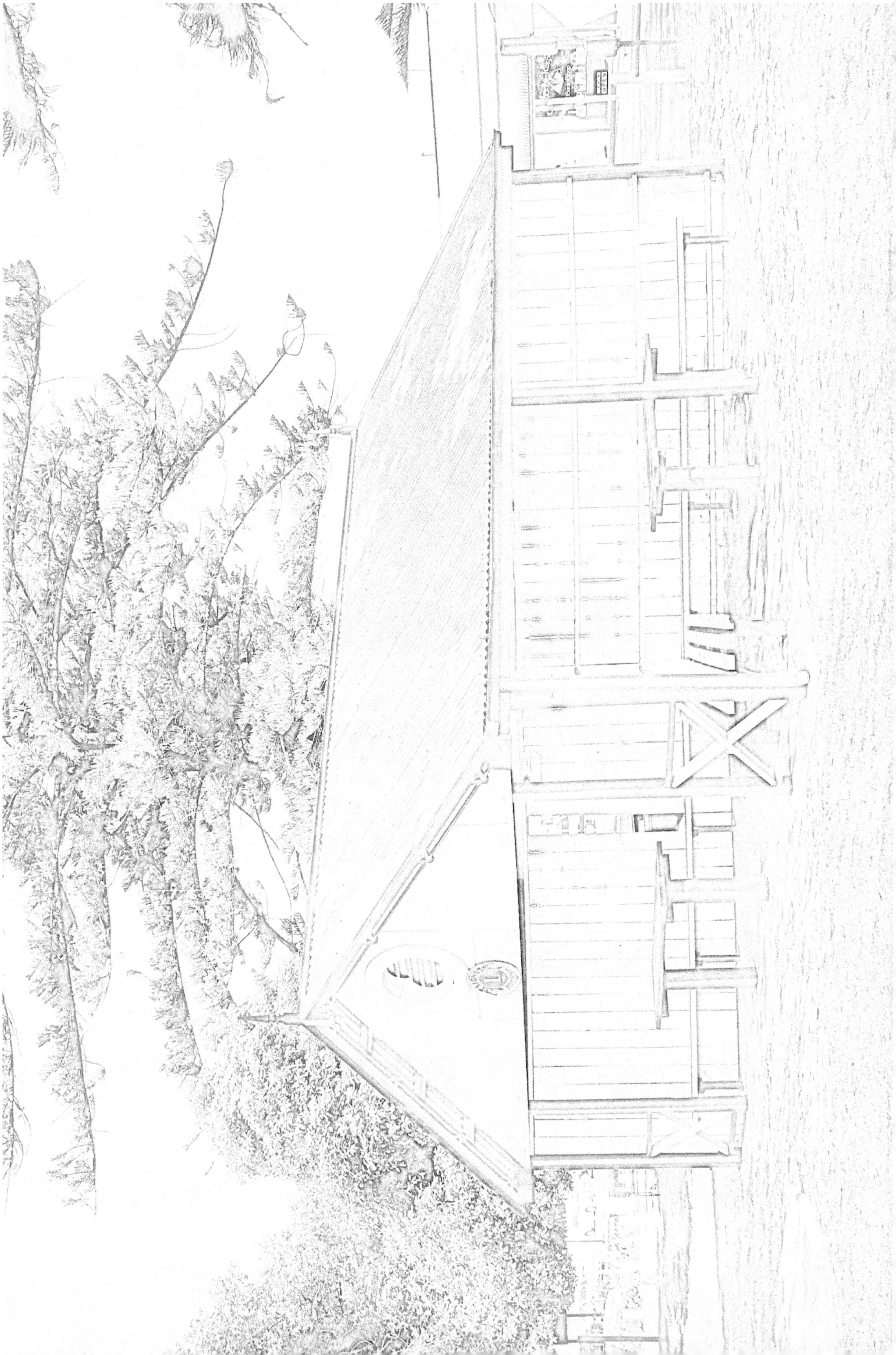

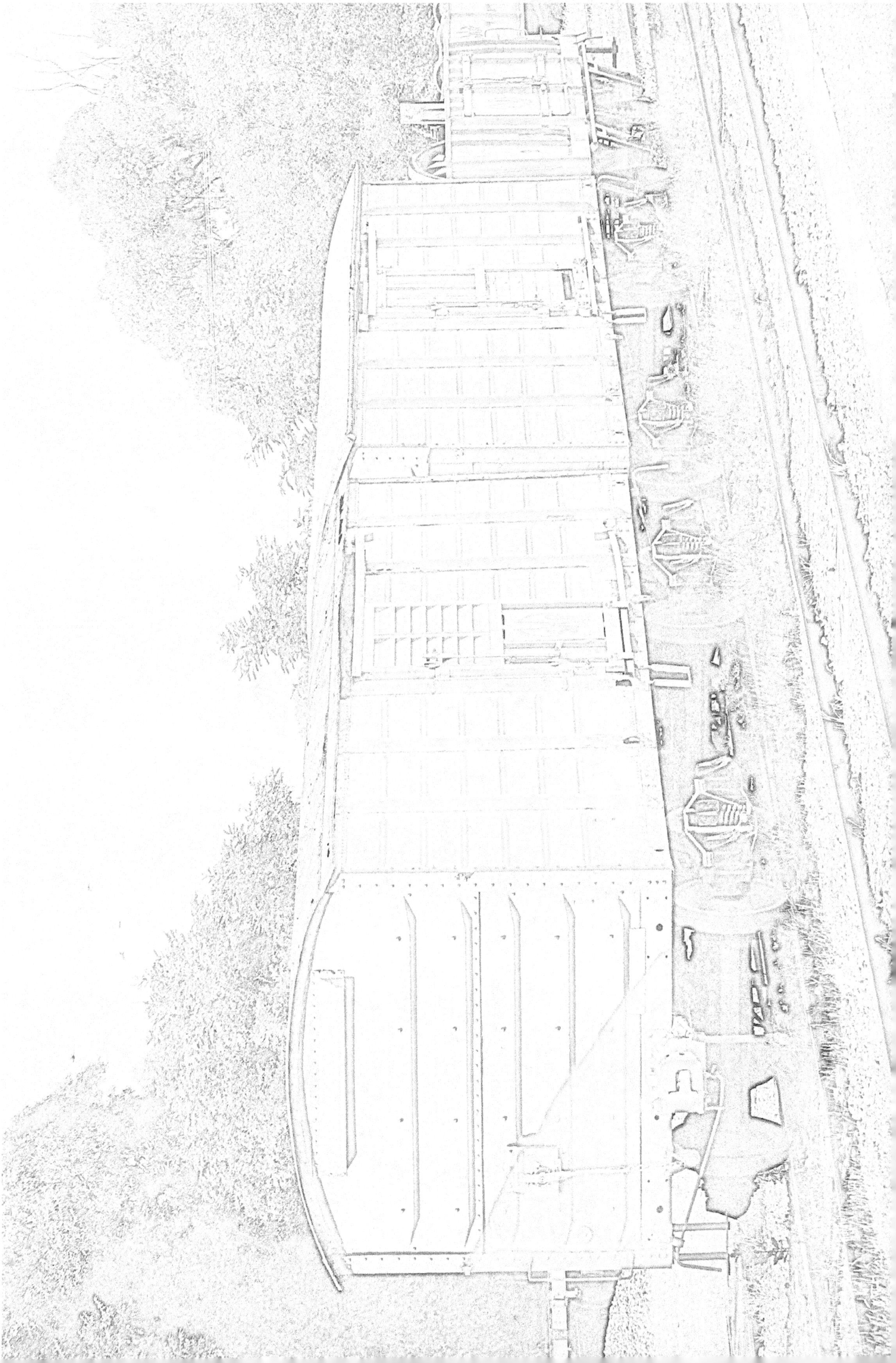

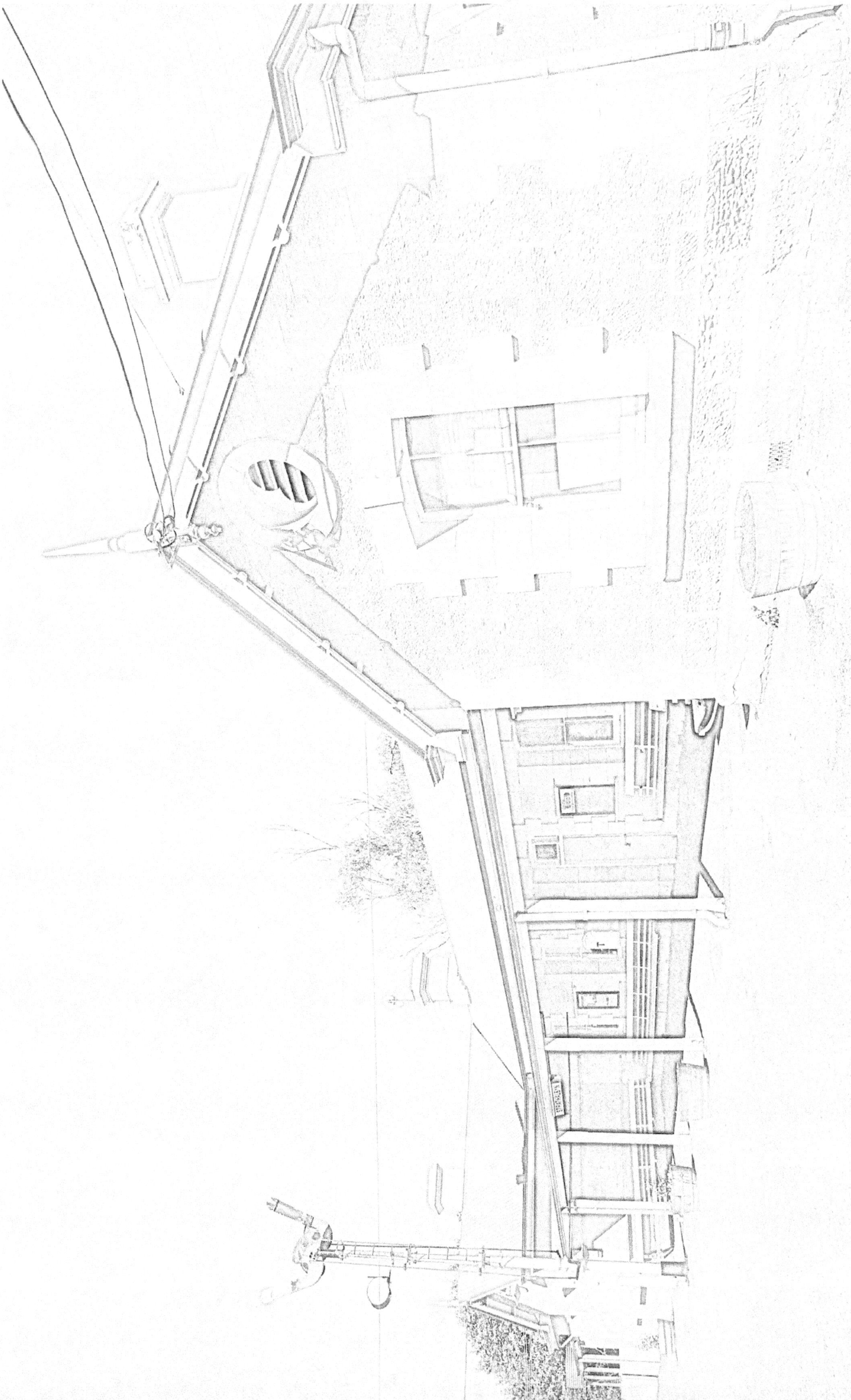

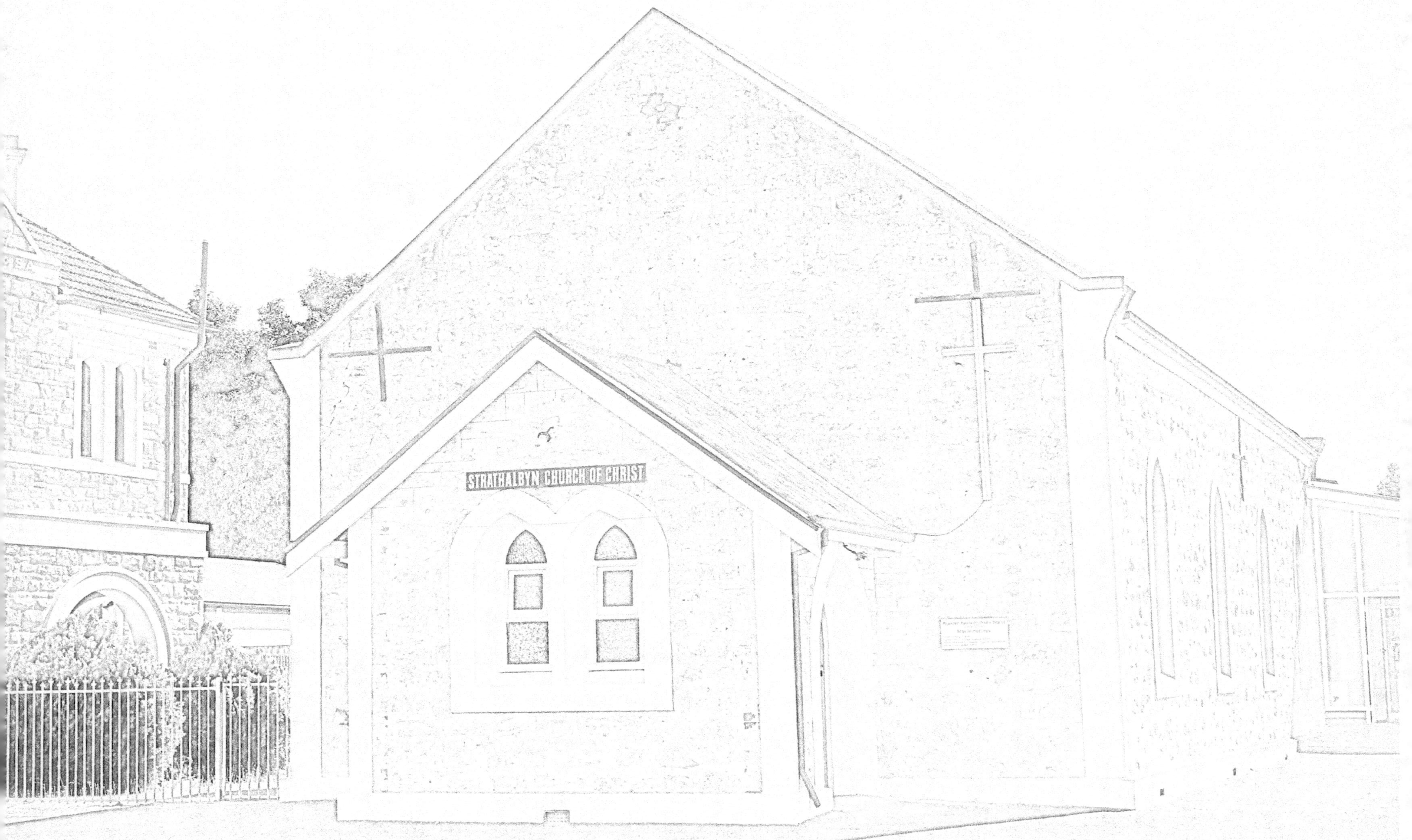
STRATHALBYN CHURCH OF CHRIST

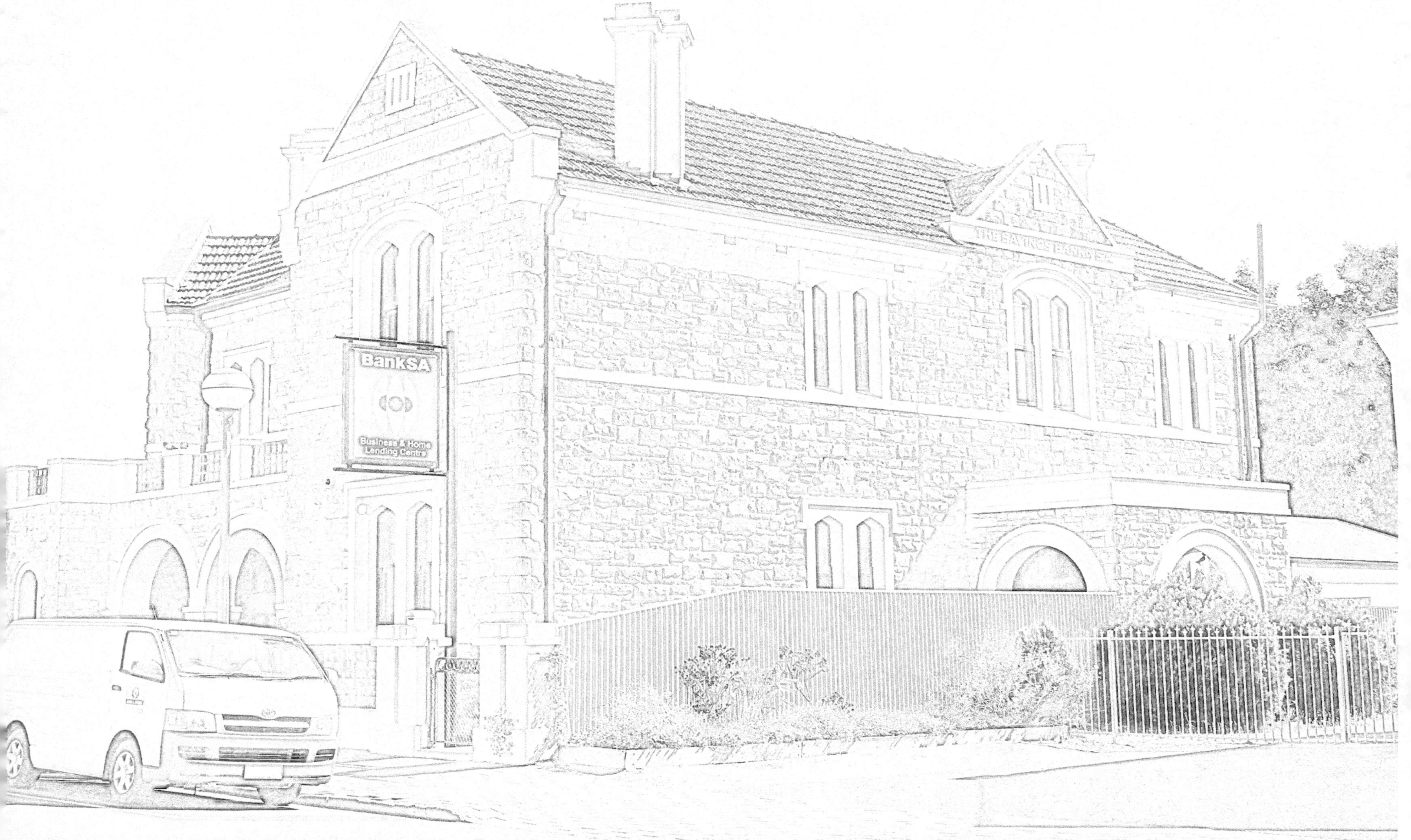
BankSA
Business & Home Lending Centre
THE SAVINGS BANK OF S.A.

www.ingramcontent.com/pod-product-compliance
Lightning Source LLC
Chambersburg PA
CBHW081100180526
45170CB00005B/1828
* 9 7 8 0 3 5 9 9 7 2 2 7 2 *